Better Homes and Gardens®
Vegetables & Herbs

You Can Grow

BETTER HOMES AND GARDENS BOOKS

Editor: Gerald Knox
Art Director:
   Ernest Shelton
Associate Art Director:
   Randall Yontz
Production and
Copy Editors:
   David Kirchner
   Paul S. Kitzke
Garden and Outdoor
Living Editor:
   Beverly Garrett
Garden Book Editor:
   Steven Coulter
Associate Garden Editor:
   Douglas Jimerson
Vegetables & Herbs
You Can Grow Editor:
   Michael Kressy
Senior Graphic Designer:
   Harijs Priekulis
Graphic Designers:
   Faith Berven
   Rich Lewis
   Sheryl Veenschoten
   Neoma Alt West

CONTENTS

Backyard Food Growing

Machines are everywhere, and they do everything from exploring outer space to picking and sorting the food we eat. Automation, of course, means release from drudgery — from the slavery of menial work. But we pay a price. We don't get to walk anymore through a meadow glistening with dew, or stoop to touch a warm tomato ripening in the sun. Machines have a way of insulating us from the good earth. Recent years, however, have seen a return to the soil.

Thousands have turned to gardening, and thousands more are thumbing through seed catalogs for the first time. Somehow, shuffling among the weeds leads to a feeling of wholeness, of becoming a part of nature and its infinite mysteries.

When you raise food crops, you become acutely aware of the sun, rain, and most of all, the life-giving soil. These are nature's elements that you work with, and sometimes battle, to produce nutritious vegetables for your table. Success brings an age-old satisfaction that goes back to the days when there were no supermarkets to fall back on. Growing your own foods is the best way possible to get a sense of seasons, of the natural cycles of the earth. The rhythm of sowing, growing, and harvesting can be just as valuable to your well-being as the vitamin- and mineral-rich harvest you eat, freeze, or can.

Ecology-conscious gardeners will tell you, too, that when they eat their own food they know *exactly* what, if any, chemicals were used in its production. Today, when the chemical question is being examined, foods known to be pure are reassuring.

In this book, you'll find all the information you need to realize your gardening dreams. A comprehensive encyclopedia section listing over 40 different vegetables offers detailed instructions on how to grow each crop. Sections dealing with soil, composting, and planting fill you in on all the basics. Included, too, are hundreds of tips on how to get your plants to grow bigger and better with a minimum of fuss. An extra bonus is an information-packed section listing the popular herbs and how to grow them.

It's worth remembering, however, that there are few hard and fast rules for growing things. What works for one gardener may spell disaster for another. This is because soil and climate conditions are different

depending on where you live. The best gardener is the creative gardener who sows in step with his own drummer. Get to know the basics, and before very long, your backyard garden will be spilling over with enough palate-pleasing vegetables and herbs to feed both your family and friends.

Planning Basics

Getting Started

Spring is full of delightful surprises. But for the gardener who dreams of a halcyon garden brimming with luscious vegetables, too many surprises can reduce the vegetable patch to a tangle of nagging chores. The best way to prevent disaster and at the same time make the most of your garden space is to carefully plot what you hope to grow and where you plan to grow it.

Where to Put the Garden. The first thing to consider is location. Vegetables need sun and lots of it. Warm-season crops such as melons, corn, and tomatoes need at least six hours of unhindered sun each day for maximum growth. Cool-season vegetables, which include the root crops (beets, carrots, parsnips, radishes, rutabagas) and the leaf crops (lettuce, spinach, mustard, chard), can get by in less sun or even shade.

If space permits a choice, keep the garden well away from trees whose roots absorb so many nutrients that vegetables simply can't compete. Remember, too, that close proximity to the house is sometimes the best defense against marauding woodchucks, rabbits, and crows. Plan to arrange your rows so that they run from north to south in order to provide equal exposure to the sun. Taller crops like corn and pole beans ought to be located on the north side of the garden where they will not cast a dense shade over your smaller sun-loving plants.

Perennials are practically worth their weight in gold to the home gardener because they poke up through the soil every spring, offering years of abundant yields. But asparagus, rhubarb, and other perennials should be given a preferred spot that is relatively free of traffic and undisturbed by plow or tiller.

Before setting pen to paper, sit down with the family and determine who likes what and how much. Nothing dampens your enthusiasm quicker than a lukewarm reception to your hard-won yields. The next step is to calculate how many plants of each vegetable are needed to keep the kitchen well-supplied. Study a good seed catalog where varieties and amounts of seed needed per row are listed.

Some plants require much more room than others with respect to their yields. This space-to-yield ratio is an important consideration, especially if space is scarce. Corn, while high on the list of vegetable favorites, is not a very efficient crop when it comes to the number of ears produced per square foot of garden. Tomatoes, on the other hand, will produce pound after pound of delicious fruit on only a few square yards of garden space.

Cool- and Warm-Season Crops. A critical element in gardening is proper timing. There are long-season and short-season vegetables, and crops that do better in the cooler temperatures of spring.

Long-season crops are those that take the entire season to grow, flower, and produce mature fruit. Melons, winter squash, potatoes, tomatoes, corn, cucumbers, pumpkins, peppers, and eggplant fall into this category. Short-season vegetables practically explode out of the ground, which means several plantings can be made within a single season. Radish, beans, lettuce, beets, and carrots can be sown and harvested before the season is half over.

Cool-season crops can be planted as early in the spring as you can work the soil and include radish, asparagus, beets, broccoli, Brussels sprouts, cabbage, carrots, cauliflower, celery, Swiss chard, chives, leeks, lettuce, onions, parsley, parsnips, peas, potatoes, rhubarb, spinach, and turnips. Warm-season vegetables, on the other hand, must be planted well after the threat of frost has passed. These include beans (green and lima), corn, cucumbers, eggplant, muskmelon, peppers, pumpkins, summer squash, winter squash, tomatoes, and watermelon.

Keeping Records. Because the memory will fade over winter, it's a good idea to keep records of what you did and how you did it. Simply write down in a notebook the crops and varieties grown, the amount and date planted, and the amount and date harvested. Remember to leave ample space for your own comments.

After a few years of careful note-taking, you'll be your own best expert. In addition, you'll be able to correct next season's mistakes early, before catastrophe occurs. Keeping track of the varieties you grow will give you the chance to experiment with different plantings. Eventually you'll hit on the right ones for your soil and climate conditions. At the same time, the record of planting dates will make future seed ordering and garden planning infinitely easier because you'll have a clear idea of what has to be done and when.

A Word About Tools. One of the beauties of gardening is that little is needed in the way of tools and equipment. If you have visions of growing a good portion of what you eat, you'll probably want to purchase a rotary tiller or small garden tractor. Breaking ground for a large garden is just too much to ask the lower back to bear. The basic hand tools you'll need include:

A long-handled hoe. The most fundamental of all the garden tools, the hoe has the widest range of uses. It's handy for breaking up clods, cultivating the soil, removing weeds, and making furrows.

A steel rake. Consisting of closely set tines attached to a long handle, a rake is indispensable for smoothing the soil and making a seed bed.

A watering can. A watering can or garden hose with a specially designed spray nozzle is welcome relief to plants when the weather gets hot and dry. Under no circumstances should you use watering devices for applying herbicides or other weed killers. Buy separate applicators so plants aren't accidentally ruined.

A garden hose. Just leaving the garden hose out in the yard after watering is easy, but to get the longest life from your hose it's best to coil it up and store it between waterings. There are several hose reels, stands, and hangers available—or you can make your own. To eliminate kinking the hose at the faucet, use a gooseneck connector that swivels with the hose.

Twine and a measuring stick. A useful tool for keeping vegetables spaced and aligned properly, the measuring stick is simply a 4-foot stake notched at 1-foot intervals.

Sprayers. Even though bugs may not yet be a problem, time can be critical if they do appear. Keep a small hand sprayer nearby so garden pests can be quashed.

Working With Soils. Soil is a lot more than just dirt. Strictly speaking, soil is the uppermost layer of the earth's surface that supports plant life. As such, it not only provides a medium to anchor plant roots, but also functions as a repository of nutrients. An understanding of soil and what it does is essential if you want to get the most from your garden. At the same time, there is a lot you can do to make your soil better for growing vegetables. (For tips on improving soil structure, see Composting, page 62.)

Nitrogen, phosphorus, and potassium are the basic nutrients plants need for good health. Nitrogen helps promote leaf growth and is essential for cell respiration and reproduction. Available from the atmosphere and the soil, it is especially helpful to crops grown primarily for their leaves, such as lettuce, spinach, chard, and cabbage. The quickest way to get needed nitrogen to plant roots is to apply a chemically prepared fertilizer. But overapplication can do more harm than good: encouraged to produce more and more leaves, the plant will be slow to blossom and bear fruit. Tomatoes, for example, can become so busy making leaves that they won't bear any fruit at all.

Unfortunately, nitrogen from most chemical fertilizers disappears rapidly from the soil unless a specially formulated "slow release" material is used. Organic materials are not as convenient to use and may be a little harder to come by, but when applied, their nitrogen remains in the soil for a much longer time. Some organic sources

of nitrogen are blood meal, cottonseed meal, fish scraps, bone meal, and cocoa shells.

Phosphorus keeps the all-important process of photosynthesis going and contributes to good fruition and healthy root systems. A key element in chemical fertilizers, phosphorus does not leach out of the soil as quickly as nitrogen. For organic sources of this element, try ground phosphate rock, bone meal, fish scraps, or cottonseed meal.

pH and What It Means. Truckloads of fertilizer will be wasted on your garden unless the pH reaction of your soil falls within the proper range. The pH is nothing more than a numerical symbol that tells you how acid or alkaline your soil is. The pH scale ranges from 0 (acid) to 14 (alkaline) with 7 the neutral point. Most vegetables do best between 5.7 and 6.9, which means your soil should be slightly acid.

But pH levels can have other consequences. Soil, which contains thousands of microscopic organisms, functions as a kind of factory where organic matter is broken down. At the same time, the soil actually breathes as rainfall pushes air out of its pore spaces and drainage sucks air back in. This constant movement of water produces a kaleidoscopic array of chemical changes. Plants send out root hairs by the millions into the nooks and crannies of the soil where they absorb nutrient ions that have become suspended in water. Hence, the vital importance of rainfall and soil moisture.

Here's where pH enters the picture. If the soil is too acid, not only will soil organisms perish, but the nutrient ions will not dissolve as readily. The end result is an infertile soil. And more and better fertilizer won't help because the right chemical conditions are just not there. Likewise, if the soil is too alkaline, certain elements will build up to toxic levels and poison plants.

How To Gauge pH. When it comes to judging the chemical condition of your soil, avoid guesswork. The most accurate method of determining pH reaction is to test your soil with a soil testing kit designed especially for the home

gardener. Available from garden supply centers, the kits contain a number of preparations that, when mixed with a soil sample, will tell you not only the pH reaction, but also the nitrogen, phosphorus, and potassium levels.

Sometimes it's possible to roughly gauge soil acidity by carefully observing how well certain vegetables grow. Beets and onions, for example, are particularly sensitive to overly acid conditions and will grow poorly, while potatoes planted in alkaline soil will be practically useless because of rampant scab disease. It's best to rely on the sophisticated methods of a soil testing laboratory. Call your county extension office for the name and address. Then simply pack off a soil sample in an unbreakable container along with a note indicating the location and depth of the sample, the kinds of fertilizers that have been used, and the crops you intend to grow. In return, you'll receive a complete analysis plus recommendations for soil amendments.

How to Change pH. Don't be put off by the chemical gymnastics of soil. Luckily for the home gardener, there are materials that will correct pH reaction easily and efficiently. Agricultural lime applied at the rate of 5 to 6 pounds per 100 square feet of garden area will raise an acid soil approximately one point on the pH scale (from 4.5 to 5.5, for example). If additional amounts are necessary, split the applciations into two doses, one at the beginning of the season and the second at the close of the season. Be sure to spread limestone as evenly as possible so no clumps remain. If possible, use a spreader built especially for this purpose, then rake the limestone into the upper 6 inches of the soil.

In regions of abundant rainfall, the soil is usually acid. But in other areas, alkaline soils are the rule. To correct an overly alkaline soil, apply powdered sulfur at the rate of 4 pints of powder per every 100 square feet of garden space. Again, rake it thoroughly into the soil. Both ground limestone and powdered sulfur are concentrated materials, so take care that plants aren't set back by over-zealous applications.

7

Plan to Boost Yields

A quick-growing, cool-season crop, mustard will do well in space vacated by cabbage.

When space is in short supply, there are a number of ways you can get more for less simply by making wise use of your garden area. The trick is to become as familiar as you can with the various needs of different crops. Then, like fitting together the pieces of a jigsaw puzzle, custom-fit crops to your garden for maximum yields. When setting seeds, keep these space-saving ideas in mind:

Vertical Gardening. Vegetables that grow on long, rambling vines, such as melons, cucumbers, and pole beans, are space guzzlers. But they're just as happy growing up as growing out and around, and may, in fact, do better that way: fruits are off the ground and are therefore cleaner, easier to pick, and probably more disease-free. If you don't have a sunny fence or trellis, construct a tepee-like support and plant seeds at the base of poles. Remember— maturing fruit will become much too heavy for the vine and will break off if not supported. Make slings out of netting or discarded nylon stockings, and tie the heavier crops such as cantaloupe, watermelon, and squash to fencing or stakes.

Interplanting. Space-conscious gardeners are constantly on the lookout for unused patches of soil, especially in the beginning of the season when seedlings require so little space. Rapid-growing

Compact lettuce plants, which mature in a matter of weeks, will thrive as young asparagus shoots start to take hold.

Let onions share the cabbage patch, but pull them before cabbages grow too large.

vegetables such as radish, lettuce, spinach, and scallions can be planted and harvested well before long-season varieties like cabbage, broccoli, squash, tomatoes, or corn begin to demand more room. Keep in mind, too, that the leaf or salad crops are somewhat shade-tolerant and will thrive even in the partial shade of larger, companion plants. Also, flower gardens often look bleak before perennials are blooming. Green and ruby red lettuce varieties can be attractive border plants.

Succession Planting. Some vegetables grow so fast that in no time their supply is exhausted and the family gardener is faced with a blank space of garden that rapidly fills up with weeds. The solution is to succession-plant for a continuous harvest. Start by planting short rows, keeping additional space in reserve for later sowings. Since lettuce can practically explode out of the soil, start off with a single 20-foot row or two 10-foot rows. When young plants are up and fairly well established (usually about 14 days after planting seed), start a new row. In another 14 days, sow a third row and continue sowing until frost puts an end to the growing season. Other quick-growers suitable for succession planting are radishes, mustard, chard, beans, and spinach. Or you can plant all at once and rely on the time requirements of different varieties to provide a continuous harvest. Tomatoes, corn, cabbage, and melons are just some of the vegetables with varieties maturing at early-season, mid-season, and late-season dates.

Second-Cropping. Because certain vegetables do better at different times of the season, it's often possible to increase yields by following one crop with another. Peas, for example, definitely do best in the cooler temperatures of early spring (or late fall). Since they require, at most, 68 days to harvest, plenty of time is left in which to grow another cool-season crop such as beets, carrots, broccoli, cauliflower, spinach, Swiss chard, parsnips, or turnips.

As soon as the first crop has been picked clean, remove old vines and remaining weeds, recultivate the area with a hoe, and rake smooth. Then mark rows with twine, dig furrows, and plant seeds. If midsummer drought threatens, cover rows with a thin mulch of dried grass clippings to preserve moisture. Chances are, enough fertilizer will be left over from the previous crop to make further applications unnecessary.

Then, in the fall when everyone else is putting their garden to bed for the winter, you'll be enjoying a bonus crop. Some vegetables even taste better after being nipped by a mild frost. Others can survive the winter if nestled under a generously applied layer of mulch. Winter-over parsnips, turnips, rutabagas, and some leaf crops for tasty treats well before the next regular gardening season begins.

A record holder for quick growth, radishes will be up before corn is knee-high.

Plotting Your Garden

Once the grip of winter is broken, nothing can stop the force of spring—not even a negligent gardener who has failed to put growing plans in order. In no time, the soil will be ready for preparation as the threat of frost fades from memory. If proper plans aren't made beforehand, spring can turn out to be a headache instead of a time for joy and expectation.

No matter how wintry things may seem just beyond the windowsill, it's never too early to think about the kinds of crops you want to grow. Besides, curling up with a seed catalog brimming with sun-splashed photos of succulent vegetables can take some of the sting out of winter.

The first step is to sit down with pencil and paper and make a list of the vegetables you want to grow. Be sure to take into account the likes and dislikes of the rest of the family so you're not left with piles of unwanted produce. Then consider some of the space-saving and yield-boosting techniques such as companion planting, succession planting, intercropping, and second-cropping (see Planning Basics, page 6). If this is your first time out, you may have to brave the cold to measure the actual space available for your vegetable garden.

Be as accurate as possible. It may require some extra calculations, but considerable money and time can be saved when you know exactly how much room you have to work with. Then transfer your measurements to a sheet of graph paper so that the sketch matches— to the inch—what you have outside. All that remains is to mark the location of the rows and the vegetables that will occupy them. Don't forget to leave space for succession-plantings of quick-growing crops. And also indicate what varieties you plan to squeeze in between rows of other vegetables.

The 25x25-foot garden plan at right may appear a trifle more complicated than the average garden but that's because it is designed to yield much more. Every inch of space is put to work. This garden, which was actually tilled, planted, maintained, and harvested, produced a whopping 270 pounds of tomatoes, 107 pounds of beans, 66 pounds of cabbage, and 149 green peppers—not to mention basketsful of lettuce, onions, edible podded peas, and spinach. And all this didn't come tumbling down at once; almost half of the total yield was picked in the fall when most gardens are idle. Here are some of the tricks that made this garden so successful:

Crop Placement. Almost all vegetables can be grouped according to how well they tolerate cool or warm weather. Tomatoes are somewhat fussy and will not produce well if temperatures are constantly low. The same is true for vine crops such as pole beans, melons, eggplant, and peppers. In our suggested plan, all have been grouped together to simplify cultivation, planting, and maintenance, and also to allow for second-cropping.

At the same time, some vegetables have been doubled up in order to increase row production. Radish seeds are mixed with carrots not only to mark the row and make weeding easier, but also to get extra use from the space. Onions are planted between cabbage plants, and extra-early radishes are sown between young tomato seedlings. Remember that seedling plants are spaced according to the needs of full-grown, mature plants. It'll take two weeks for the roots to spread out and become established and another two weeks for the stalks and leaves to begin demanding more room—plenty of time to squeeze in a harvest of lettuce or radish.

Second-Cropping. Wherever an early-yielding vegetable is likely to leave part of the garden vacant, a second vegetable has been scheduled to take its place.

Braided onions hung up to dry are an attractive addition to the pantry door.

Cabbage, for example, will be up and out by midsummer. So a fall crop of Oak Leaf Lettuce and Tendergreen mustard is planted in its place. Lettuce, spinach, and peas also are quick growers and are followed by three rows of turnips. Beets, carrots, and beans all can be followed by midsummer plantings of the same vegetables or other fall season crops.

Varieties. With careful choice of different varieties, the tomato patch not only can produce a near-avalanche of fruit, but also will yield sun-ripened tomatoes from mid-season all the way to the first frost in fall. Big Boy tomatoes, which ripen in 78 days, and Rutgers (74 days) are mixed with Early Girl variety, which is ready within 54 days. But all gardens aren't square, and not everyone likes the same vegetables. Growing methods necessarily vary according to your particular tastes, as well as the gardening space you have to work with. The key is to get acquainted with the ins and outs of growing things so that you can adopt what appeals to you and discard the rest. The end result will be hours of enjoyment and bushels of vitamin-rich vegetables.

A Green zucchini or Summer Crookneck squash
B Nantes Half Long carrots with Sparkler radishes (mix seeds together so both grow in row)
C Black-seeded Simpson lettuce followed by Just Right turnips
D Bloomsdale Long-Standing spinach followed by Just Right turnips
E Ruby lettuce followed by Just Right turnips
F Dwarf Gray Sugar edible-pod peas
G Parsley and basil
H Chives
I Eggplant*
J Tokyo Bell peppers*
K Stringless Green Pod beans
L Early Wonder beets
M Shallots*
N Early White Vienna kohlrabi
O Roquette followed by onions from seed
P Dwarf Blue Curled Vates kale
Q Onions*
R Red Acre cabbage*

S Early Jersey Wakefield cabbage* or broccoli* (onions planted between)
T Danish Roundhead late cabbage* (onions planted between; Oak Leaf lettuce and Tendergreen mustard replace cabbage mid-season)
U Surecrop Stringless wax beans (two rows planted 6 inches apart; buy two packs of seed)
V Straight Eight cucumbers (two rows planted 3 inches apart)
W Romano pole beans (two rows 3 inches apart)
X Rhubarb chard (sow in clumps 6 inches apart)
Y Burpee's Big Boy tomatoes*
Z Early Girl tomato*
AA Rutgers tomato*
BB Yellow Pear tomatoes*
CC Patio tomatoes*
DD Roma tomatoes*
EE Small Fry tomatoes*
FF Comet radishes between tomatoes
GG Existing rhubarb
HH Flowers   *Buy started plants or sets

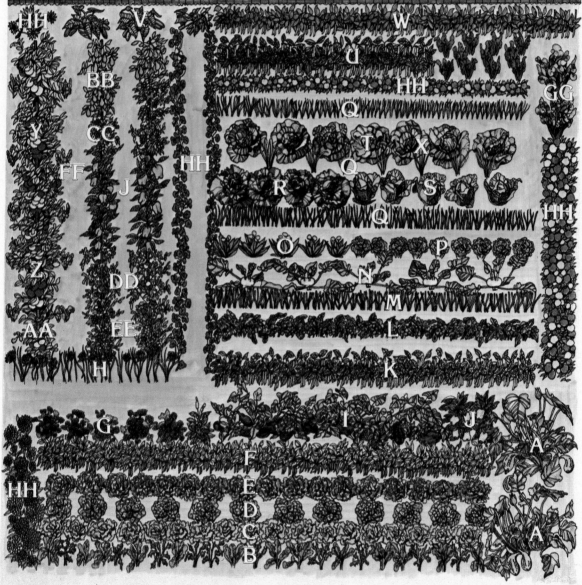

11

With planning, vegetables can be grown almost anywhere. Here a bumper crop thrives in a raised bed bordered with railroad ties.

Gardening on a Long, Narrow Space

Fortunately for the backyard gardener, homegrown vegetables don't have to take center stage. If the backyard is already committed to landscaping or a play area, look for an out-of-the-way location for the vegetable patch. A long, narrow strip along the back or side of your property is all that's needed. Take a careful look at unused spaces surrounding the house or the garage. Sometimes a strip of vegetables can be tucked into an area between buildings, along the back of a garage, or beside a driveway or path.

Always keep in mind the three crucial elements for successful growth: soil, sun, and water. Soil not only provides physical support, but also acts as a nutrient bank where the plants' food can be stored within reach of the roots. A good soil also will allow for the free drainage of excess water while retaining just enough for plants to have a continuous supply. Sun and plenty of it is the second top requirement. As a general rule, vegetable plants need at least six hours of unobstructed sun each day. Finally, water makes it possible for the roots to absorb nutrients clinging to soil particles. Too much, however, can suffocate and kill the plants.

Don't despair if your soil looks like it will only grow stones. Many a lifeless garden has been turned into Babylonian splendor through a simple program of soil improvement. If your soil stays soggy and wet because of poor drainage, consider installing inexpensive drainage pipe, or building raised beds from discarded railroad ties, stones, or staked planks. When choosing a site next to the house or garage, remember that the soil may be filled with building trash and large rocks. Chances are the topsoil either has been carted away or used elsewhere on the property. In any event, some soil amendments are a must.

One of the best ways to bring a stony, sandy soil up to snuff is to incorporate organic material that is partially or completely decayed. Leaf mold, compost, or aged manure mixed with hay are excellent. Spread a 3- to 5-inch layer of shredded leaves over the garden area and work it thoroughly into the top 6 inches of soil. If manure is used, be sure large clumps are broken up or removed. Peat moss, spoiled hay, and lawn clippings are other suitable additives.

Providing soil for a raised bed means starting from scratch, unless topsoil is hauled in from another location. When mixing your own, use equal amounts of soil, sand, and peat moss. Lime, rock phosphate, cottonseed meal, or other organic sources of nutrients can be added initially or later. Chemical fertilizers shouldn't be applied until just before planting. Mix materials thoroughly and allow them to settle in beds before sowing seed or setting out any new plants.

Two things are worth remembering when working with raised gardens. First, the soil tends to dry out quickly because it's farther from subterranean water supplies. While the ground-level garden can get by on one thorough watering per week, the raised bed will need water at least every other day—if not every day—during hot spells. And second, the soil will compact more easily, which means you should avoid walking on it whenever possible. Use a wide board when planting seed or weeding between rows.

Here are some tips for planting vegetables in narrow gardens or alongside buildings.

Remember, plants need air. Buildings, fences, and walls tend to obstruct the free flow of air which causes protected gardens to be somewhat warmer and also more susceptible to unwanted fungus diseases. To improve air circulation, give crops a little more room than you would in an open, exposed vegetable garden.

Since space is at a premium, consider broadast-sowing, as

Carrots have a good space-to-yield ratio, making them ideal for cramped quarters.

opposed to stringing seeds out single file. Simply dig a furrow 4 to 6 inches wide and scatter seed, allowing for proper spacing.

Because the side of a house, garage, or fence will reflect a fair amount of sun, garden temperatures will be greater. Coupled with lower air circulation, added heat makes it much more difficult to grow cool-season vegetables such as lettuce, spinach, beets, or chard. For best results, concentrate on the warm-season crops such as melons, cucumbers, squash, tomatoes, and eggplant.

Grow compact varieties. In recent years, great strides have been made in developing vegetables that

require less and less room in which to grow. Plant the bush varieties instead of long, rambling vines.

Grow up instead of around. If vine crops are a must, use poles, racks, string, fencing, or whatever other material is at hand as support. Be sure to support the heavy fruit from trellis-grown vines with a net or cloth sling. This will prevent the fruit from falling from the vine.

With careful planning and a little extra effort, your narrow garden will produce as well as any. And remember, a sun-ripened tomato from the south side of the garage tastes just as good, if not better, than the tomato plucked from the middle of a fifty-acre tomato farm.

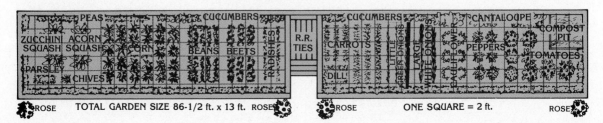

PEAS CUCUMBERS CUCUMBERS CANTALOUPE
ZUCCHINI ACORN CORN BEANS BEETS R.R. TIES CARROTS LITTLE GREEN ONIONS LARGE WHITE ONION CAULIFLOWER PEPPERS COMPOST PIT
SQUASH SQUASH RADISHES
PARSLEY CHIVES DILL TOMATOES

ROSE   TOTAL GARDEN SIZE 86-1/2 ft. x 13 ft. ROSE   ROSE   ONE SQUARE = 2 ft.   ROSE

A Dooryard Garden

Too often the gardener forgets that after all is planned and planted, whether or not fresh vegetables end up on the dinner table really depends on the family cook. All the vitamin-rich produce you reap isn't going to mean much if the rest of the family has little or no interest in what's happening in the backyard vegetable patch.

One way to spark interest is to plant a dooryard garden by the kitchen door. Juicy red tomatoes, succulent wax beans, and cucumbers mixed with just the right herbs will prove too tempting to pass up. And the convenience of fresh carrots, greens, or radishes at arm's length from the sink will inspire the cook to greater gourmet heights. There are other advantages, too. Small animals, wary of all the kitchen door traffic, will give the garden a wide berth. At the same time, maintenance will be simplified because tools and water hose are nearby. And those pesky weeds that sprout overnight can be nipped on your way to the garage or mailbox. But best of all, gardening pleasures can be shared by the whole family.

The suggested plan below consists of four 10x10-foot sections separated by stone, gravel, or brick walkways for easy access and maintenance. All areas can be reached with a hoe or rake as well as the all-important watering can. If the soil appears beyond repair, consider raised beds of old railroad ties, cinder blocks, or staked planks. Whatever shape your garden takes, the important thing is to arrange your crops so ripe vegetables can be harvested without unnecessarily trampling and compacting the soil.

Because space is limited, the dooryard garden has to be something of a monument to gardening efficiency. Note the plan: vegetables that lend themselves to vertical growth, such as cucumbers and pole beans, are planted to one side where their vines can be trained on twine or specially constructed trellises. Tomatoes, which will sprawl in all directions if not kept in check, are grown inside wire mesh cylinders or cages.

Besides benefiting from vertical growing, yields also are boosted by making sure that every inch of soil is kept in continuous production. Early-maturing peas are cleaned out as soon as the last pea pod is picked, and are replaced with a sowing of warm-season beans. The same is true of radishes and spinach. Lettuce, kale, and carrots are similar quick-growers that can be followed by other crops.

A dooryard garden wouldn't be complete without herbs. Here basil, thyme, tarragon, and chives are interplanted with the vegetables. Many can be potted up for winter.

A dooryard garden just steps away from the kitchen will produce bushels of tasty vegetables and herbs from spring to fall.

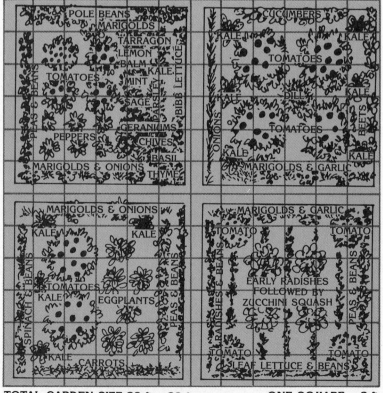

TOTAL GARDEN SIZE 23 ft. x 23 ft.   **ONE SQUARE = 2 ft.**

Food Among the Flowers

Flower fanciers need not rule out those delicious vegetables. Vegetables have blossoms, too, and some are as exquisite in shape and color as the most prized of ornamentals. Eggplant, for example, produces large, bell-shaped lavender blooms of outstanding beauty.

Remember, too, that flowers aren't everything. Since background plantings are as important as the main attraction, expert gardeners are just as interested in factors such as leaf color, shape, and texture.

When it comes to leaves and unusual growth habits, vegetables have outstanding qualities of their own. Ruby lettuce or red cabbage make excellent border plantings, while carrots, parsnips, and turnips have lace-like leaves. Rhubarb with its broad leaves and bright red edible stalks is especially eye-catching. Even some of the vine plants such as pole beans or cucumber can offer striking contrasts when trailing over a wall.

Rhubarb, chard, and sunflower offer interesting flowers and leaves. Foxglove, above, lends color.

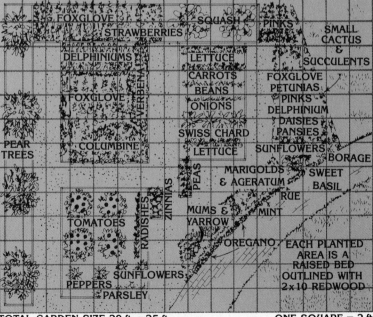

TOTAL GARDEN SIZE 29 ft. x 25 ft.   ONE SQUARE = 2 ft.

Bumper Crops From A Big Lot

The idea of living off the land is as old as man himself. Gardeners everywhere are making connections with the good earth by growing as much of what they eat as possible. If you have the land and don't mind a little extra work, plan a bumper crop from a large garden.

The advantages of thinking big are numerous. To begin with, you have enough room to grow the highly rewarding perennial crops

JUNE BEARING STRAWBERRIES
GRAPES
JUNE BEARING STRAWBERRIES

EVER BEARING RED RASPBERRIES

ASPARAGUS

MARIGOLDS

POTATOES

ONIONS

BROCCOLI & BEETS

ONIONS

SWISS CHARD

KALE

CARROTS & RADISHES

EARLY CABBAGE, LATE CABBAGES WITH ONION SETS

MARIGOLDS

SPINACH

SPINACH

POLE LIMAS

DOUBLE ROW OF PEAS ON CHICKEN WIRE FENCE

LEAF LETTUCE

BUTTER CRUNCH LETTUCE

1st CROP CORN AFTER PEAS

2nd CROP CORN AFTER PEAS

EVER BEARING STRAWBERRIES

MARIGOLDS

BUSH ACORN SQUASH

BUTTERNUT SQUASH

BLUE HUBBARD SQUASH

MARIGOLDS

DILL

BUSH PUMPKIN

MARIGOLDS

DWARF SALVIA

MARIGOLDS

CANTALOUPE

PEPPERS

GREEN BEANS

WAX BEANS

TOMATOES

CUCUMBERS

GREEN BEANS

BUSH ACORN SQUASH

WATERMELONS

SUMMER SQUASH

CHILDREN'S GARDEN

SALVIA

ONE SQUARE = 3 ft.

such as asparagus and rhubarb. Even better, you can devote part of the garden area to growing small fruit. The joy of homegrown strawberries, raspberries, or grapes is one your family will long remember. A larger garden also means you can spread out your harvest by growing plenty of vegetables to store for use in the winter. Potatoes, pumpkins, and the various winter squashes—too space-demanding for small gardens—are excellent storage crops for winter use.

Additional space also means you can set out an extra row or two of family favorites for pickling, canning, or freezing. Or, a sliver of soil can be set aside for experimentation—planting that intriguing vegetable you've always been curious about but never had enough room to grow. And don't forget the kids: a large garden also lets the children get in on the fun of setting seeds to soil.

The main requirement of planting for larger yields is soil that is in tip-top shape. Don't waste money, effort, and time by trying to guess what's in your soil. Remove a plug of soil from several locations, allow it to dry, and sift it to remove large stones and roots. Then place a small amount in a non-breakable container, label it accurately, and call your county extension office for the location of the soil testing laboratory to which you should send it. In return, you'll receive a complete analysis.

Remember, too, that your soil needs more than just chemicals. Try to work in soil conditioners such as rotted manure, compost, and other organic materials. A green manure —winter rye, for example—planted in the fall and plowed under in the spring can do wonders.

At first glance, you might think a larger garden only means more wear and tear on the lower back. But proper planning, judicious use of mulches, and a little help from a rotary tiller can make a big garden just as easy to manage as a small one. For warm-season crops, nothing beats black plastic as a mulch. Spread it between rows of corn, melon, cucumber, and tomato. Hay, lawn clippings, and shredded leaves also can be used in place of the plastic.

And then, of course, there's water. Most vegetables require at least one inch per week.

Yields can be doubled by keeping the soil busy. Here, onions are planted between cabbages, while marigolds improve appearances and may discourage bugs.

A must for the large garden are the popular Brassicas: cauliflower, cabbage, Brussels sprouts, and broccoli. Shift sites each year to prevent disease.

Melons, cucumbers, and other vine crops need warm days and nights for good yields. Black plastic mulch combined with straw will boost growth and cut down maintenance chores.

Intensive gardening using raised beds and high-density planting can boost the average yield by as much as five times.

Gardening Intensively

If you can get all the elements together—from the tiniest nematode to just the proper balance of wind and rain—vegetables will practically gush out of the ground. The trick is to manage a natural harmony in which plants, soil, bugs, bacteria, seeds, leaves, and even the moon work to help each other. That's the aim of a time-tested method called intensive gardening, which was originally developed in France. Two basic techniques are involved:

Raised Beds. Ecology-conscious gardeners, sensitive to the vast complexities of soil, take great pains to juggle the components of their soil so plants get everything they need. The raised bed (see page 20), created by double-digging and adding sizable amounts of compost and organic fertilizers, offers better aeration and water retention, deeper root penetration, and more numerous soil organisms.

High-Density Planting. Because the soil is so much richer and is prepared to twice the depth of the ordinary garden, more plants can be squeezed into each square foot. For example, instead of growing carrots in space-wasting rows, they are sown at 2-inch intervals in all directions (see diagram below). Once plants become established, the leaves are so dense and close

together that a natural mulch is formed. As a result, moisture is held in and weeds are deprived of sunlight.

Few things in life are free, and the luscious vegetables that spill out of a bio-dynamic, high-density garden are no exception. Double-digging is hard work, especially the first time around. But the advantages far outweigh the temporary inconvenience of soil preparation. Here's how it's done:

Stake out a bed that is any length, but no more than 5 feet wide. Narrow beds let you reach all plants from walkways, eliminating one of the worst gardening problems, soil compaction. Starting at one end, dig a trench across the bed about 12 inches wide and 12 inches deep. Cart topsoil to the opposite end of the garden. Then loosen the subsoil at the bottom of the trench by inserting a shovel and wiggling it back and forth. Start the second trench. This time, place the removed topsoil into the first trench. Repeat this procedure until you get to the end of the bed. The topsoil carted to the opposite end now can be used to fill in the final trench.

Intensive gardeners boast that 20 percent of their soil is organic matter, which means additives are worked in at the outset. Before double-digging, spread a layer of

Turnips planted leaf-to-leaf are almost self-weeding when leaves shade the soil.

compost over the entire bed. Let the soil rest for a day and then add bone meal (¾ pound per 100 square feet), wood ashes (1 pound per 100 square feet), and rotted manure (2 bushels per 100 square feet). Work it into the top 6 inches of soil with a spading fork. Because of the added air and organic matter in the soil, your bed should be from 4 to 6 inches above ground level when you finish. Taper the sides so rainfall won't wash soil away. On new beds, pull the soil into a ridge around the perimeter of the garden.

When ordering seeds, plan on companion planting so crops can help each other. Tomatoes, for example, are said to do better when sown with carrots, chives, onion, or parsley. Cucumbers thrive with beans, corn, peas, or radishes, but dislike close proximity to potatoes and aromatic herbs.

Remember that rows are taboo in intensive gardening; they waste space, invite soil compaction, and reduce possible yields. Seeds should saturate the bed in all directions. Once sprouts have appeared, thin to desired distances. But be sure to allow plants to grow close enough together to form a leaf canopy over the soil. In short, leaves should just touch one another. The experts plan their yields so that an entire bed will be harvested at one time. Succeeding crops are then planted as soon as the bed can be reworked. Or, you can enjoy a continuous harvest throughout the growing season by succession planting. Make repeated sowings of lettuce, peas, and spinach.

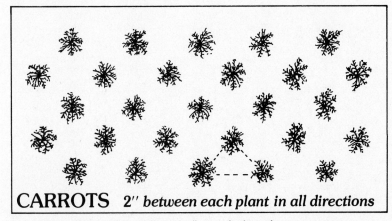

CARROTS *2″ between each plant in all directions*

In broadcast plantings, thin seedlings to allow each plant adequate growing space.

Gardening in Raised Beds

Of the three crucial elements in gardening—sun, soil, and water—good soil is often the hardest to come by. Today, an unfortunate companion of building progress is the acres and acres of sterile asphalt that result. Even soil in traditionally agricultural regions is losing ground because of mismanagement. But don't shelve your gardening dreams too hastily. One way around the problem of poor or nonexistent soil is to make your own.

Raised beds filled with specially mixed soil are a special bonus to vegetables for a host of reasons. To begin with, you have almost complete control over the drainage, porosity, moisture retention quality, and organic composition of the soil. In addition, you can custom-make the beds to fit the various nooks and crannies of your backyard. And you'll soon discover how easy raised beds are to care for. Because soil is ideal, plants are healthier and less-bothered by insects and

Raised beds can solve a knotty soil problem and also enhance your home's landscaping.

Constructed of treated 2-by 8-inch boards, raised beds can hold the ideal soil for each vegetable you grow.

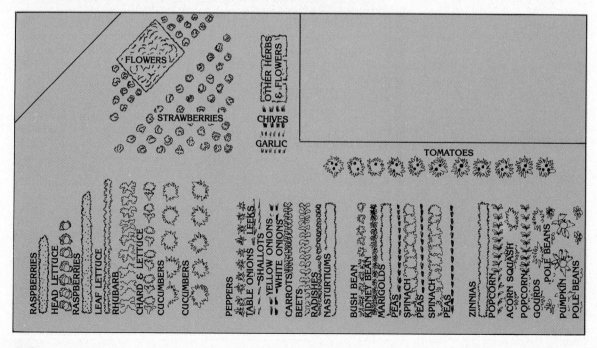

Ideally spaced and well-maintained walkways make weeding and cultivating chores much simpler, and with lovely results.

disease. Weeding and cultivation are easier because beds are accessible from all sides. And harvest is a snap because raised plants are easy to get at and don't require excessive stooping and bending.

How you build your retaining walls and the material you use are limited only by your imagination. Bricks, cinder blocks, old railroad ties, or treated planks are a few of the possibilities. Just be sure to locate the beds where they can benefit from at least six hours of sun per day. Walkways should be covered with pea gravel, coarse sand, or bark chips. If wood is used, be sure to treat it with a copper sulfate preservative; other chemicals may be toxic to plants.

Soil is where it all begins, so take extra care in supplying the very best available for your raised vegetable garden. If beds are small, you can save time by using a synthetic soil available at most garden supply centers. These are lightweight mixes made of organic material and expanded minerals and fortified with fertilizer. Some gardeners prefer to go it alone by thoroughly mixing together equal amounts of peat moss, sand, and garden soil. Or you can take the existing soil and bring it up to snuff by adding the proper amounts of compost, peat moss, sand, fertilizer, and limestone. Soil reclamation means a little more work, but the satisfaction is well worth it.

Since raised beds mean reduced space, choose those vegetables that produce greater yields per square inch of soil. Root crops, including beets, carrots, parsnips, turnips, and radishes, should head the list. When scanning your seed catalog, keep a sharp eye out for bush varieties as opposed to trailing vine types.

A word about care: as with soil in containers, raised beds tend to dry out much faster than regular soil. Be sure to keep a watering can or garden hose nearby, especially during hot, dry spells. Chances are, plants will need a thorough daily watering in drought weather. Or better still, install a drip irrigation system for low-maintenance watering.

Gardening in Containers

One of the beauties of soil is that it can be picked up and moved. Or if soil isn't available, you can simply mix your own or buy bags of scientifically formulated growing medium. All of which means that you don't need acres and acres of land to enjoy fresh vegetables. Potatoes will thrive in a bushel basket, tomatoes will grow happily in hanging baskets, and lettuce will produce lush green leaves in a window box.

Anything that will hold soil can be used as a container. Old kitchen pots, cake pans, plastic hampers, wood baskets, clay pots, or even an old sink will do. If you have scrap lumber, you can make your own containers. The mobile mini garden pictured on the next page is easy to build and light enough to put on wheels. Overflowing with salad crops such as lettuce, chives, cherry tomatoes, radishes, and bunching onions, the unit can be kept in full sun all day. The 6-foot troughs constructed of treated wood are filled with a lightweight, commercially prepared soil mix.

Whatever you put in your containers, keep these critical requirements in mind. One of the primary functions of soil is to give roots something to hold onto so plants can stay upright. And the windier it is, the heavier the soil should be. For example, if you envision a grove of eggplants on top of a 30-story building, plan on deep containers weighted with an ample supply of soil.

Container soil also dries out quicker because, unlike topsoil, it can't soak up moisture from the water table through capillary action.

Easy-to-build wooden tubs lined with plastic or tin are perfect for crops.

Ordinary chicken wire nailed to a wooden frame provides support for the roving vines of Kentucky Wonder beans.

Therefore, water at least every other day (every day during dry, hot spells), and make sure the soil you use is high in water retention ability. Peat moss, perlite, vermiculite, and rotted compost can hold considerable amounts of water. Sand, on the other hand, holds practically no water.

For small amounts of container soil, your best bet is to purchase specially prepared mixes from a garden supply center. Investigate, too, the synthetic soils available. All have been carefully developed to provide everything plants need for good growth. For larger amounts, you might consider mixing your own. The basic ingredients are equal amounts of garden loam, peat moss, and coarse builders' sand. If your garden soil is on the sandy side, you may want to reduce or eliminate the sand portion. Dump materials into a single pile, then shovel into two or three successive cone-shaped piles to mix the soil thoroughly.

The advantage of pre-prepared mixes is that they are sterile and free from soil-borne diseases. Although garden loam can be sterilized by heating, it's a messy, time-consuming process. If a sterile medium is needed for starting seedlings and you want to mix your own, use equal parts of peat moss, vermiculite, and perlite. This starter mix has no nutrient value, however,

Clay pots filled with nutrient-rich soil make excellent containers for vegetables.

so a balanced fertilizer will have to be added once seedlings have become established.

Here's a sampling of crops suitable for container growing.

Tomatoes. Without a doubt, tomatoes offer more per cubic inch of space than any other crop. With dozens of varieties available, you can pick and choose the variety that appeals to your tastes. For starters, try salad or cherry tomatoes. Small in size and compact in growth habit, these cherry-sized tomatoes do especially well in hanging baskets. And large varieties are easy to grow providing the container is big enough to accommodate larger root systems.

Lettuce. A cool-season crop that can tolerate partial shade, lettuce not only offers different-textured leaves with unusual color, but is easy to grow. The loose-leaf types are preferable because outer leaves can be picked as they develop while the main plant is allowed to remain and produce additional leaves. Other leaf crops suitable for container culture are Swiss chard, spinach, mustard, collards, roquette, and dandelion.

Cucumbers. Because of their vines, cucumbers can be attractive patio or terrace plants in addition to a delicious salad ingredient. To save space, train plants on a trellis or other support. Since cucumbers are heavy feeders, your containers should be capable of holding plenty of soil. Mix in generous amounts of rotted compost or manure.

Potatoes. A bushel basket spilling over with potato vines is an eye-catcher that also can be fun for the whole family. In the fall when vines begin to die off, fresh spuds can be dug for a delicious dinner-time treat. To increase your yield, use a taller container and hill plants as they develop.

Carrots and Beets. Root crops are perfect for containers because they take up so little room. Just be sure your soil is deep enough to hold roots. And when ordering seeds, look for shallow-rooted carrot varieties.

Eggplant. Another warm weather crop, eggplant seems to enjoy container culture. Start seeds indoors several weeks before the last expected frost.

Detail of corner construction shows a caster attached to bottom of the frame.

Stepped 1x8 wooden troughs are nailed securely to the 2x6 frame.

This mini garden on wheels, constructed of treated wood, makes an ideal salad garden. The rack can be turned at the touch of a finger, which means crops can get full sun all day. Plastic nailed to the top protects plants from cold and direct sun.

23

ABCs of Vegetables

Whether or not your garden overflows with delectable vegetables ultimately hinges on how well you get to know the particular cultural needs of your crops. In this section, you'll find all the information you need. These vegetable entries, arranged in alphabetical order, give you planting how-to and cultural tips for the recommended varieties, plus information on how and when to harvest them.

Most, if not all, of the vegetables listed can be grown anywhere in the United States. But remember, weather conditions are crucial. Temperatures and average frost dates can vary from one neighborhood to the next, depending on terrain and the placement of the garden. Contact the nearest United States agricultural county extension office for reliable advice on planting times in your area.

A

ARTICHOKE (GLOBE)

A gourmet delight, the globe artichoke is grown for its tender, delicately flavored flower buds. Because of their inability to survive cooler temperatures, artichoke plantings are not often found in northern gardens.

VARIETIES: Green Globe is the standard variety.

PLANTING: A perennial that can produce succeeding harvests for as long as four years, artichoke is usually started indoors. When all danger of frost has passed, the young plants are set out in the garden, allowing 4 feet between rows and plants. These initial plantings will not bear fruit until the following season. However, side shoots may be removed with roots intact and planted in another section of the garden for late-summer harvest.

CULTURE: A deep, well-prepared soil with plenty of nutrients and an ample supply of moisture—especially when buds first begin to form—can mean a yield of 12 to 16 buds per plant. Before planting, fortify the soil with generous amounts of rotted manure and commercial fertilizer. After plants are established, numerous suckers will appear at base of stems. Remove weaker shoots, allowing 5 or 6 to remain for later transplanting.

After the first killing frost in the fall, cut stems 1 foot from the ground. In regions where frost penetrates deeply, protect root crowns with a heavy but porous mulch. In spring, remove mulch and treat emerging plants to a dose of manure and fertilizer.

HARVEST: As soon as flower buds are visible, check plants daily so that buds can be picked just before petals begin to spread open.

ASPARAGUS

Launching an asparagus bed requires a little extra in the way of planning and soil preparation, but the rewards are easily worth the effort. The average bed can be expected to yield tender, succulent spears for at least fifteen years, while some asparagus patches have been known to produce for one hundred years.

VARIETIES: The recommended varieties are the Washington strains, which are resistant to asparagus rust.

PLANTING: With an abundance of care, good timing, and patience, asparagus may be started from seed. But in terms of work expended, it's far more economical to obtain one-year-old crowns from a reputable nursery. Starting young plants also means the shoots can be harvested that much sooner. Dig a trench 16 inches deep, then refill with 10 inches of soil enriched with generous amounts of manure, compost, or fertilizer. Tamp soil, place crowns about 18 inches apart, and cover with several inches of soil. As the plants grow, fill in the trench with additional soil. By the end of the first season, plants will have reached soil level. Rows should be spaced 3 to 5 feet apart.

CULTURE: Asparagus is a heavy feeder and should be given yearly doses of fertilizer or nutrient-rich compost or manure. Because weeds compete for food, the bed should be carefully cultivated and mulched. Hoeings or harrowings, however, must be kept shallow to avoid injury to asparagus roots. In the fall, after plants have died back, remove stalks to prevent disease spores from wintering over. This also is a good time to spread a mulch, which will improve the soil as it discourages next season's weeds.

HARVEST: The best spears are no more than 8 inches long, with tight, compact tips. To prevent injury to roots and other emerging spears, break off shoots when picking. As with corn and peas, asparagus should be picked quickly upon ripening to preserve maximum flavor and sweetness. Brand-new beds started with crowns need at least a year, but full harvest won't be realized until the third year. Allow the young plants to develop strong, well-structured root systems.

B

BEANS

Beans not only offer exquisite flavor, but also provide the venturesome gardener with a seemingly endless variety of types and sizes. There are beans for frying, boiling, sauteing, drying, baking, and even stringing. Most beans are tender and must not be planted until the soil has warmed and all danger of frost has passed.

VARIETIES: Depending on how they are used, beans fall into two categories: edible-podded varieties and the shell or tough-podded types. The edible-podded or snap beans are eaten, pods and all, before they are fully grown. Beans also vary according to their habit of growth. Bush beans grow low to the ground and do not require support. Pole beans, on the other hand, produce lengthy vines and must be supported with poles, a trellis, or fencing. Popular varieties of bush beans include Contender, Resistant Cherokee (wax), and Tender Crop. Among the pole bean varieties, the most well-known is Kentucky Wonder.

PLANTING: In order to supply the dinner table with a continuous harvest of beans, plan on succession-planting every two weeks. However, the large, tender seeds are susceptible to rot if sown in soil that is cool or overly moist. Space rows 24 to 30 inches apart, with seeds placed 2 to 3 inches apart. Pole beans should be planted in hills 2 to 3 feet apart. Since the pole varieties generally require a somewhat longer growing season, they are not as adaptable to succession plantings. Lima bean seeds are especially sensitive to cool, wet conditions and should not be planted until after the soil has warmed. Rows should be 24 to 30 inches apart, while plants should stand 8 inches apart. Pole varieties can be planted five seeds to a hill spaced 3 feet apart. When seedlings have emerged, thin to three plants per hill. Six- or seven-foot stakes driven into the ground next to each plant will provide sufficient support. Keep in mind that climbing vine plants are excellent for planting along a fence or trellis. Plenty of sun and well-drained soil are the major requirements.
CULTURE: Beans are adaptable to a wide variety of soil conditions and require little in the way of care beyond the customary removal of invading weeds. If the soil is light and sandy, a supplementary application of a complete fertilizer

will stimulate growth (use 3 pounds of a 5-10-10 fertilizer per 100 square feet of garden area, or use a fertilizer compounded particularly for vegetables). However, do not allow fertilizer granules to come into direct contact with plant leaves or stems.
HARVEST: Once the seed pods begin to develop, keep careful track of their growth, since overripe snap beans are tough and stringy. Pods should be picked before seeds swell enough to cause visible bulges in their shells. Try to stay out of the bean patch when plants are wet; simply brushing against leaves can spread virus diseases.

BEETS

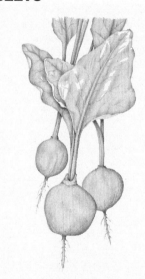

Some gardeners insist that the best parts of beets are their tender, flavorful greens which can be prepared and eaten in the same way as spinach. Whatever your preference, beets are a double-bonus crop because both roots and tops make delectable additions to any menu. The red-veined, deep-green leaves are also quite decorative, making beets a natural for patio, container, or border plantings.
VARIETIES: The tried and tested varieties include Crosby, Early Wonder, and Detroit Dark Red. But other varieties offer yellow or elongated, turnip-shaped roots. Early Wonder matures in about 55

days; winter or storage beets in about 80 days.
PLANTING: As with most root crops, beets require a finely prepared soil in which to form well-shaped roots. When working the soil in the spring, be sure to remove all stones, roots, and other obstructions. A cool-season crop, beets can be planted as soon as the soil can be worked. Furrows should be about ½ to 1 inch deep, with rows spaced 12 to 20 inches apart. Since each seed is really a clump of smaller seeds, sow no less than 1 inch apart in the row. If soil tends to crust, cover seed with a mixture of sand and peat moss or leaf mold.
CULTURE: The key to successful beet growing is rapid growth and the proper soil pH level (between 6.5 and 7.0). The first requirement is achieved by ample watering. Soil acidity can be corrected by applying sufficient amounts of ground dolomitic limestome (about 5 pounds per 100 square feet).
HARVEST: Because seeds are clusters, the seedlings will appear in fairly dense clumps. When plants are about 4 inches high, thin to 3 inches apart. The removed plants should go right to the dinner table. The second thinning, after beets have grown to a height of 6 to 8 inches, will give ample room for roots to form. Usually, the tops of the beets will become visible as harvest time approaches. If they don't, simply push away enough topsoil to determine root size. Ideally, roots should be 1½ to 2 inches in diameter for maximum tenderness and flavor.

BROCCOLI

The easiest to grow of the brassicas (cabbage, cauliflower), broccoli contains an abundance of vitamins. The heads continue to form even after the central flower cluster has been cut, offering a continuous supply for the dinner table. The brassicas, however, are perennial victims to a variety of root diseases, the most devastating of which is club root. The best defense is to avoid planting them in the same place twice.

VARIETIES: The best-known varieties are Green Sprouting and Waltham 29. A recent hybrid is Green Comet, which produces tight, compact heads and matures in about 55 days.

PLANTING: Because broccoli thrives during the cooler temperatures of spring and fall, it's best to start seed indoors or to purchase healthy plants from a reliable nursery or garden supply center. After young plants have been acclimated to outdoor conditions (a two-week stay in a cold frame will do the trick), plant in the garden 18 to 24 inches apart. Be sure to wrap aluminum foil, cardboard, or stiff paper around the stems of each plant as protection against cutworms. At least 1 inch of the collar should be below the soil line, with 2 inches above.

CULTURE: A large part of successful broccoli-growing hinges on ample moisture. If plants don't have to struggle on insufficient moisture, stems and blossoms will remain deliciously tender. If a dry spell threatens, spread a mulch around plants and between rows, after applying a vegetable or balanced fertilizer to each plant. Also, spray plants at weekly intervals with *Bacillus thuringiensis* to combat cabbage worms.

HARVEST: Once buds begin to form, keep careful track of growth so that heads can be picked at peak flavor. Heads should be no more than about 4 inches across; small, compact heads are best. Under no circumstances should the tiny flowerets be opened. Leave side shoots for later pickings.

BRUSSELS SPROUTS

The Brussels sprout plant produces a tower of miniature cabbages that cling to the upright stem like coconuts. Like broccoli, Brussels sprouts provide a continuous crop. As lower sprouts are harvested, upper ones continue to develop.

VARIETIES: The most reliable varieties are Jade Cross and Long Island Improved.

PLANTING: Since Brussels sprouts require a long growing season, it's best either to start plants indoors 6 to 8 weeks before the last frost in spring, or to purchase healthy seedlings from a garden supply center. Try to select a garden area not formerly used for any of the other brassicas (cabbage, cauliflower, or broccoli) to help combat club root disease. As soon as the ground can be tilled and prepared, set plants in the row 18 to 24 inches apart. Be sure to provide a collar around the stem of each plant for protection against cutworm attack.

CULTURE: The early stages of growth are when plants require the most nutrients. Brussels sprouts will benefit from side-dressings of a complete fertilizer or well-rotted compost when plants are about 8 inches high, and every two weeks thereafter. When sprouts begin to grow at leaf axils (where leaves join stems), break off lower leaves. The small, cabbage-like sprouts will continue to grow up the stem. Spray plants at weekly intervals with *Bacillus thuringiensis* to combat cabbage worms.

HARVEST: The best sprouts are compact and about 1 inch in diameter. Buds that have been allowed to overdevelop become loose and eventually are susceptible to invading bugs. Use a sharp knife to cut off sprouts, leaving enough trunk so that new sprouts can grow. Approaching frost is no cause for concern, since Brussels sprouts improve in flavor after a light frost or two. Once harvest has been completed, remove plants and destroy to minimize the chance of disease the following season.

C

CABBAGE

Easy-to-grow and adaptable to a wide variety of soils, cabbage not only lends itself to a host of mealtime uses, but also offers a fascinating choice of types. Some, like the Savoy, have attractive, crinkly leaves, while others form compact heads. If space is a problem, red cabbage mingles nicely with landscaping plantings either out in the open or along borders. Then there are the long-season and short-season varieties. In short, whatever your soil conditions, there is a cabbage that will do well for you.

VARIETIES: Early: Jersey Wakefield, Golden Acre, and Market Topper. Mid-season: Burpee's Copenhagen Market and Marion Market. Late-season: Danish Ballhead, Penn State Ballhead, and Savoy. Recommended red cabbage varieties include Ruby Ball and Red Acre.

PLANTING: A decidedly hardy crop, cabbage can be planted in the garden as soon as soil conditions will allow. Most growers, however, like to get a jump on the season by starting the seeds indoors six to eight weeks before outdoor planting time. After at least two weeks of hardening-off in a cold frame, the plants can be set out in rows 24 to 36 inches apart with about 14 to 24 inches between each plant. Like fellow brassicas, cabbage is easy prey to club root disease. The best defense is to keep brassicas continually on the move by planting them in different locations each season. Be sure to place a collar around the stem of each plant to foil cutworms.

CULTURE: For succulent heads, keep plants well supplied with moisture throughout the growing season. Since roots also like to be on the cool side, many gardeners spread a 3- to 4-inch layer of mulch around the base of plants. If sawdust or other woody material is used, it's best to add additional amounts of fertilizer to counteract the possible nitrogen depletion of the soil. An excellent material that maintains soil moisture and at the same time improves soil tilth is dried cow or horse manure. Since cabbage is grown for its greens, side-dressings of nitrate of soda at transplanting, and every four weeks thereafter, will improve the crop. Keep fertilizer granules from coming into direct contact with stems or leaves. Spray at weekly intervals with *Bacillus thuringiensis* to combat cabbage worm attack.
HARVEST: Heads should be picked when still tight and compact. Cracking occurs during dry spells when the plants cannot get sufficient moisture. The remedy is to supplement rainfall with thorough drenchings from the garden hose. Some gardeners reduce cracking by severing roots on one side of the plant with a thrust or two of a sharp spade. When harvesting, cut stems with a sharp knife near the base of the plant.

CARROT

Few vegetables can match the carrot when it comes to greatest yield per square inch of garden soil. A prolific grower that's easy to care for, the carrot is easily among the top ten vegetable favorites.
VARIETIES: The key to well-formed roots is well-prepared, obstruction-free soil. But if shallow soil is a problem, grow stubby varieties such as Royal Chantenay or Scarlet Nantes. Medium-sized varieties include Pioneer and Nantes Half Long. The best-known of the regular varieties that produce long, tapering roots are Trophy, Gold Pak, and Imperator.
PLANTING: The key requirement for a bountiful carrot crop is thoroughly prepared soil that has been well-supplemented with nutrient material. All clumps, sticks, stones, and miscellaneous debris should be removed to prevent roots from becoming misshaped. Plant seeds fairly thinly, about ½ inch deep, in rows spaced 12 to 18 inches apart. If ground tends to bake and form an impenetrable crust, cover seeds with shredded sphagnum moss or vermiculite instead of garden soil. Since carrot seed takes its time to germinate, it helps to mix rapidly germinating radish seed right in the packet. The early-sprouting radishes will mark the row and make it possible to stay ahead of weeds.
CULTURE: When carrot seedlings have emerged, thin carefully to one plant every 3 inches. The row should be thinned a second time to 6

inches between plants. Carrots from these thinnings can be a delightful mealtime addition served raw in a salad or slightly cooked. For a continuous supply, sow at three-week intervals. Carrots, however, are a cool-season crop and will not do well in the height of summer heat.
HARVEST: A big carrot is not necessarily the best carrot. Size in vegetable-growing is not a good indication of worth, since overgrown produce is often tough and mealy. Carrots are no exception. Pick when tops of roots are about ½ inch in diameter for best flavor.

CAULIFLOWER

Some people who love to eat cauliflower avoid planting this tasty vegetable simply because they think it is hard to grow. Yet the effort needed to grow cauliflower is hardly more than that required for broccoli or the ever-popular tomato.
VARIETIES: The best-known and most reliable are the Snowball types. Also of high quality are Burpeeana and Snow Crown. The purple varieties have the distinct advantage of not requiring blanching. The heads develop a natural purple color that turns to green when cooked.
PLANTING: Most gardeners start cauliflower plants indoors in order to take advantage of the cooler temperatures of spring and early summer. Once the plants have been hardened-off, they may be planted in rows 24 to 30 inches apart with plants spaced 20 to 24 inches apart. Be sure to protect stems from cutworm damage by supplying 2-inch-wide collars of stiff cardboard or aluminum foil. Protect tender transplants from the direct rays of the sun with boards or heavy paper.

CULTURE: For solid, well-formed heads, cauliflower requires cool temperatures, plenty of moisture, and frequent fertilizing. Soil should be well-prepared and supplemented with ample amounts of manure or rotted compost. Additional side dressings of a nitrogen-rich fertilizer are helpful once plants have become established. If drought conditions threaten, supplement rainfall with thorough drenchings from the garden hose. However the moisture is supplied, it should be equal to at least 1 inch per week.

Cauliflower is a perfect candidate for mulching, since straw or hay placed around plants will help reduce water evaporation while keeping soil temperatures fairly cool. Once the flower heads or "curds" are about the size of a half dollar, the leaves should be gathered together and tied to form a protective canopy. Sunlight striking the flower bud will cause discoloring. The purple varieties do not require tying.

HARVEST: Within three to eight days of tying, the heads will have matured and become blanched. Cut stalks just below the heads. If they are overgrown, the buds will begin to open, reducing their quality.

CELERIAC

Grown for its bulbous root, celeriac has a delightful celery flavor especially prized in Germany where it is used extensively as a salad ingredient. In home gardens, celeriac often replaces celery, since it doesn't require blanching.

VARIETIES: Often referred to as "knob celery" or "turnip-rooted celery," the principal varieties are Alabaster and Marble Hall.

PLANTING: Since celeriac is a long-season crop, it's best to get seeds underway indoors. The young, hardened seedlings can then be moved to the garden as soon as the soil can be prepared. Quick growth is essential for a successful crop, so the soil should be kept moist and chock-full of nutrients. Prepare soil thoroughly, working in ample amounts of manure, compost, or other organic material. A complete commercial fertilizer also may be added. Then arrange rows 18 to 20 inches apart, with plants standing at least 9 inches apart. If starting from seed, plant in shallow furrows and cover with a thin layer of sifted soil. When seedlings have emerged, thin to 3 inches apart, and when plants are 8 to 10 inches high, thin again to 9 inches apart. Side-dressings of a high-nitrogen fertilizer may be applied at four-week intervals.

CULTURE: Keep the row free of weeds by hand-picking. When hoeing between rows, keep cultivation shallow to avoid injury to root systems. If soil begins to dry out, moisten the area thoroughly with the garden hose. Spreading a 3- to 4-inch mulch is an effortless way to control unwanted weeds and, at the same time, maintain the moisture content of the soil. If bulbs begin to push through, cover them with soil to preserve whiteness.

HARVEST: Pull plants when roots appear to be about 4 inches in diameter. With a mulch protection, the harvest may be extended into the early winter months.

CELERY

Something of a prima donna among vegetables, celery not only requires near-perfect growing conditions, but also constant attention from the gardener. However, a successful celery patch and the flavor delights of fresh celery will certainly make all the extra effort worthwhile.

VARIETIES: The most reliable varieties of celery include Emerson Pascal, Burpee Fordhook, and Utah 52-70.

PLANTING: To ensure healthy, disease-free plants, start seeds indoors for early spring transplanting. But remember—celery, just like other vegetables started indoors, requires at least a two-week stay in the cold frame to gradually become acclimated to outdoor conditions. Once the soil has been thoroughly prepared and conditioned with an abundance of nutrient-rich organic materials, the plants may be set out in rows 24 to 30 inches apart. Plants should stand 6 to 10 inches apart in the row. If possible, choose an overcast day for transplanting. But if sunshine persists, it's best to shield plants from direct rays with pieces of cardboard or newspaper. Water generously after planting.

CULTURE: Essential to successful celery-growing is rich soil, fairly cool temperatures, and a continuous supply of moisture. Nutrients can be supplied by working manure or compost into the soil when the garden is turned in the spring. Supplemental feedings should be given at regular intervals throughout the growing season. And when dry conditions threaten, ample use should be made of the garden hose. Remember, thorough waterings once a week penetrate the sub-layers of the soil, while frequent sprinklings only tantalize the plant.

In earlier days, growers used to

blanch stalks by hilling earth against plants. Blanching, however, is not really necessary and robs stalks of their vitamin content. But if white stalks are a must, simply place boards on either side of the plants and hold them in place with soil. The trick is to keep out sunlight.

HARVEST: A healthy, well-formed bunch of celery will be all of 4 to 5 inches across after outer stalks have been removed. To harvest, simply pull up plants, shake off soil, and cut off root clumps.

CELTUCE

If the demands of celery prove insurmountable, try a row or two of celtuce, a member of the lettuce family whose thick, stiff stalks have the delicate flavor of celery.

VARIETIES: Burpee's Celtuce.

PLANTING: Very hardy, celtuce has the same culture requirements as lettuce. Simply sow seeds as soon as the ground can be worked. For an early crop, plant a few seeds indoors while snow still covers the ground. Be sure to harden-off in a cold frame before setting young plants out in the garden.

CULTURE: Since leaves and stalks are the prized portions of the plant, help boost growth by keeping the soil supplied with ample amounts of nitrogen. Before planting, mix a balanced, commercial fertilizer into the soil and work in generous amounts of manure or compost. Once plants are 4 to 6 inches high, apply a side-dressing, being sure to keep fertilizer from lodging in plants. Thin rows when plants are 3 inches high, and again at 5 or 6 inches.

HARVEST: Celtuce leaves, which are said to contain four times the vitamin C as lettuce leaves, can be picked early and used in salads. If tender stalks are desired, wait until

plants have reached maturity. Pick stalks and eat either raw or cooked.

CHARD, SWISS

For gardeners whose planting activities are crimped by a shortage of available space, Swiss chard is an old standby. One planting can provide a supply of tasty greens throughout the growing season. As leaves emerge and become mature, they can be picked without injury to the plant. And as the season progresses, new leaves will quickly take their place.

VARIETIES: Among the most reliable varieties are Large White Rib and Burpee's Fordhook. For border plantings or containers, consider Rhubarb Chard, which produces dark green, crumpled leaves with deep red veins.

PLANTING: Chard will do nicely in almost any garden soil, although wet or overly moist conditions ought to be avoided. Like beets, chard will do poorly in an acid soil, preferring a pH of 6.5 to 7.5. Get chard underway as soon as the ground can be worked. As with beets, chard seeds are really clusters and can easily be over-planted if sufficient space is not provided. Dig a furrow about 1 inch deep by dragging a hoe handle through the soil and using a garden twine as a guide. Drop seeds individually into the row and space them about 1 inch apart. Cover seed with soil and tamp lightly with the back of the hoe. Rows should be about 18 to 24 inches apart.

CULTURE: The first thinning, when plants are 6 inches high, should leave plants 3 inches apart. Thin again to 6 inches, and finally to 12 inches between plants. To boost leaf growth, apply side-dressings of a high-nitrogen fertilizer. Thinnings can be prepared and served like spinach or beet tops.

HARVEST: When plants are fully grown, pick outer leaves as they mature and prepare as is, or separate the "chard" mid-rib from the leaf and serve like asparagus. If the pickings are managed properly, a single planting will last the summer. Some growers prefer to confound winter by placing protective caps over plants for pickings well into the fall. Or, the entire plant can be pulled, leaving root balls intact, and placed in a cold frame or greenhouse where it will continue to grow.

CHICORY

The gourmet gardener whose tastes have progressed beyond the common lettuces will want to try a row or two of chicory. The tender, creamy-yellow leaf clumps offer a unique flavor that is at once tangy and mild.

VARIETIES: Some chicory varieties can be grown for their roots, which are cooked and served similar to carrots. But most seedsmen list chicory under salad greens and offer varieties best suited for producing an abundance of leaves. The best-known variety of chicory is Witloof, sometimes referred to as French Endive.

PLANTING: Chicory can be considered a miniature version of Cos lettuce, and is grown in much the same way. Hardy and preferring cooler temperatures, it can be sown as early as the ground will permit. Or, plants can be grown indoors for transplanting. Rows should be 15 to 24 inches apart for best growth.

CULTURE: The object of growing chicory is to produce healthy plants that can be taken indoors in the fall where they are forced to develop blanched leaf clumps. Since leaves are the principal crop, periodically apply a nitrogen-rich fertilizer. Thin plants to 6 to 8 inches between plants. The leaves of some varieties can be picked as they mature.

HARVEST: In the fall, before the threat of frost, dig up plants and replant in boxes filled with peat moss and sand. Then place in a warm, dark place where the plants can continue to grow. Trim leaves to about 8 to 10 inches in length. In about a month, depending on the growing conditions, the Witloof can be cut. If roots are left in place, new leaves will begin to form, providing a second cutting.

CHINESE CABBAGE

Sometimes called celery cabbage, Chinese cabbage is a "must" ingredient for oriental dishes, but also can be shredded for cole slaw or used as an acceptable stand-in for celery.

VARIETIES: The standard variety is Michihli. Other varieties include Burpee Hybrid and Crispy Choy.

PLANTING: Not only is Chinese cabbage a cool-season vegetable, but if grown in warm weather, it will quickly bolt to seed and become practically useless. As a result, most gardeners plant Chinese cabbage in late summer for a fall crop. Plan on sowing seed at least three months before the average date of first frost in the fall. As with cabbage, success depends on cool temperatures and ample moisture. Rows should be 18 to 30 inches apart, with plants standing about 6 to 8 inches apart.

CULTURE: For healthy, tender leaves, be sure that sufficient amounts of nitrogen are present in the soil. At planting time, work in a balanced fertilizer and, if possible, generous amounts of compost or rotted manure. When plants emerge, supplement with side-dressings of a balanced or high-nitrogen fertilizer.

HARVEST: Pick plants before seed stalks begin to form.

COLLARDS

Chiefly grown in southern regions where cabbages seldom head properly because of higher temperatures, collards have a distinctive flavor that makes them more than a mere substitute for cabbage.

VARIETIES: The best varieties are Georgia, which improves in flavor after a light frost, and Vates, a compact, dwarf-like variety.

PLANTING: As a member of the brassica group, collards are as susceptible to club root as cabbage, Brussels sprouts, and cauliflower. Choose a different growing site each year. As with other leaf crops, rapid growth and plenty of nitrogen and moisture are of paramount importance. Sow seeds 1 inch deep as early in spring as the soil will permit. Space rows about 2 feet apart. Once plants are well up, thin to 3 to 4 inches apart. Thin again to 6 inches between plants. Thinnings make delicious additions to the dinner menu.

CULTURE: Since an abundance of tender, green leaves is the desired crop, it pays to provide a continuous supply of a high-nitrogen fertilizer. Either work it into the soil at planting time, or apply it in bands along each side of the row at three-week intervals throughout the growing season. Keep weeds at a minimum by hand-picking in the row, and frequent cultivating between rows. Remember to keep hoe penetration shallow to avoid injuring collard roots,

HARVEST: Like chard, collards can be harvested by picking the outer leaves as they develop, leaving inner leaf buds to grow for later pickings. Or the entire plant can be pulled.

CORN

To the hardened gardening pro, a garden is nothing unless presided over by tall, stately stalks of corn. Corn is a heavy feeder; it can be decimated by armies of bugs, and it definitely makes heavy demands on available space. But the rewards

of fresh corn straight off the cob are not to be trifled with. Even if it produces only a handful of stalks, every garden should have a smattering of corn.

VARIETIES: Half of the joy of growing corn is the veritable supermarket array of varieties available. There is golden yellow corn, white corn, and corn with a little of each, as well as popcorn for the kids and ornamental corn to complete Halloween festivities. Among the yellow corn varieties, the most popular are Seneca Chief, Golden Bantam, Sundance, Gold Cup, and early Sunglow. Of the bicolor types, Butter and Sugar, Honey and Cream, and Sprite are good producers. For white corn, try Silver Queen, Spring White, or Silver Sweet.

PLANTING: Warmth, moisture, and a rich soil are the crucial ingredients for a bumper crop of corn. Pick a sunny spot where the soil is rich in plant nutrients. If soil needs improvement, work in compost or rotted manure at the rate of about 2 to 4 bushels for every 100 square feet of garden area. If pH reaction is on the low side, add sufficient amounts of lime as a supplement.

Since corn is a tender vegetable, wait until the soil has thoroughly warmed before setting out seed. Block-planting (short rows forming a square) increases the chances of proper pollination. Space seeds about 8 inches apart in rows 26 to 40 inches apart. To provide an initial food supply, dig a furrow 3 inches deep and sprinkle a band of complete fertilizer along the bottom. Cover with a layer of soil, and plant seeds 1 inch below original soil level. If corn is planted in hills, sow five seeds to a hill and space hills about 4 feet apart.

CULTURE: Once sprouts have broken through, the rapidly growing stalks will require abundant amounts of food. As soon as plants are 6 to 8 inches high, begin a program of side-dressing the rows or hills with rotted compost every two weeks. Also, thin plants to three stalks to a hill, and row plants to 12 to 18 inches apart. If dry weather begins to thwart growth, provide

supplemental waterings with a sprinkler. When tassels and silks appear, keep a lookout for injurious insect pests. Corn borers, for example, like to drill their way into the base of ears or into tassel stalks. Small mounds of corn sawdust piled on leaves is a telltale sign. Either spray plants or remove worms by hand (see Pests and Problems, page 66).

HARVEST: As soon as the ear is removed from the stalk, sugars begin to break down into carbohydrates, which means that the sooner corn is cooked and served, the sweeter it will taste. As a rule of thumb, put the kettle on to boil before going out to fetch the corn. Ears are ready to be picked when kernels at the tips are plump and silks have dried out.

CORN SALAD

Small in size but chock-full of flavor, corn salad is popular among Europeans and has recently gained popularity in America. Similar to lettuce, the plants take up little room and are excellent for cramped quarters or container gardening.

VARIETIES: Available varieties are few in number, since only a handful of seedsmen carry the seeds. Best-known is Large Round-Leaved corn salad.

PLANTING: Because mature plants take up little space, they can be sown fairly close together. Plants can stand as close as 6 inches apart, with rows 12 to 18 inches apart. Like lettuce, corn salad is difficult to grow during the dog days of summer, so plan on an early spring planting, or a late summer sowing for a fall crop. As with most other greens, success

depends on plenty of nitrogenous material in the soil, together with a generous supply of moisture. At planting time, treat the soil to a high-nitrogen fertilizer or generous amount of rotted manure (about 4 bushels per 100 square feet of garden area).

CULTURE: When plants emerge and are fairly well established, thin to 3 inches. Later, thin again until mature plants are about 6 inches apart in the row. As leaves develop, sprinkle each side of the row with a light side-dressing of organic fertilizer, such as blood meal. Repeat every three weeks until harvest. If the sun becomes intense and wilting occurs, provide partial shade by placing shading material over or alongside plants.

HARVEST: Leaves may be picked as soon as they reach mature size (about half the size of a lettuce leaf). Pick outer leaves only, so that inner leaves can continue to grow for later pickings.

CUCUMBER

Once a freshly plucked cucumber has graced a family salad, the supermarket variety will seem pale by comparison. For flavor, abundance, and convenience, cucumber comes close to heading the list of the most popular home garden crops. Its trailing growth makes it a favorite among small-space gardeners who enjoy finding imaginative ways to fit the vines into their landscape.

VARIETIES: Seedsmen offer two types for home gardeners: slicing cucumbers and pickling cucumbers. Slicing varieties are developed for table use but also may be used for pickling. Gherkins are cucumbers picked when they are small; however special varieties that produce only gherkin-sized fruit are available. Chief slicing varieties are Marketmore 70, Gemini, Triumph, Burpless Hybrid, and Straight Eight. Pickling cucumber varieties include Mariner. Green Star, Wisconsin SMR 18, and Burpee Pickler. Bush Whopper is a bush variety adaptable to container growing. "Gynoecious" varieties, like Victory Hybrid, bear

mostly female flowers and frequently offer greater yields.
PLANTING: Cucumber is a tender, semi-tropical vine plant that requires plenty of warmth and a rich, well-drained soil. Although it's troublesome to transplant, some growers start seeds indoors six weeks before the last expected frost. Or, after soil has warmed and all danger of frost has passed, sow outdoors in four- or five-seed hills spaced 6 to 8 feet apart. New bush varieties should be spaced about 2 feet apart. Place a shovelful or two of rotted manure and a handful of fertilizer under each hill. Seeds should be planted no more than ½ inch deep.

CULTURE: When seedlings have broken through and developed first or second sets of true leaves, thin out weakest plants leaving three plants per hill. With proper moisture and warm temperatures, the vines will rapidly extend in all directions. It's a good idea to train cucumber vines up a fence or support to save garden space. Fruit will be kept cleaner, too. If early, solitary fruits appear, pick them off to ensure a larger yield. When the main crop begins to emerge, pick fruits as soon as they are ready so that later cucumbers are not robbed of the necessary nutrients. If the vines seem to be getting out of hand at the expense of the fruit, pinch off the outermost new growth. As the season nears an end, vines should be pinched back so that existing fruit will mature before frost.
HARVEST: If fruits are removed regularly, the vines should produce an abundant yield. Remember, nothing is saved or gained by allowing a cucumber to swell to gargantuan proportions; large fruits often become dry and pulpy. The fruits can be gathered at any stage of their development, but if their skin begins to yellow, the cucumbers are becoming overripe and should be picked.

D

DANDELION

In the lawn, the dandelion is a yearly pest, but in the garden it is a gourmet's delight, especially among salad-lovers. Wild dandelion can be included in salads, but cultivated varieties will produce more succulent leaves.
VARIETIES: Thick-Leaved.
PLANTING: Sown mostly as a spring or fall crop, dandelion can be grown in any well-drained soil, the richer the better. Use purchased seeds and plant shallow furrows (about ½ inch deep) in rows 12 to 15 inches apart. Cover with sifted soil and moisten thoroughly. Fortify soil with a balanced fertilizer, manure, or compost.
CULTURE: Keep plants thinned to prevent overcrowding. Fully grown plants should stand at least 6 inches apart. Be sure to pinch off flowers so wind-scattered seed won't infest your lawn. Other than thinning, dandelion requires little care.
HARVEST: Once leaves have matured, outer greens can be picked fresh at any time.

E

EGGPLANT

With its thick, velvety leaves and exquisite lavender blossoms, eggplant looks like an exotic, tropical plant. The fruit—large with purplish-black, shiny skin—is unlike anything else the garden is likely to produce. Indeed, it is this unique appearance that makes eggplant especially popular as a landscaping plant.
VARIETIES: Among the most popular varieties are Black Magic, Burpee's Black Beauty, and Early Beauty Hybrid.
PLANTING: Eggplant is a long-season tender vegetable whose cultivation, although similar to that of tomato, needs a little extra attention. Most gardeners either start seeds indoors eight to ten weeks before their particular frost-free date, or purchase young plants from a reliable garden supply center or nursery. Sow seeds in flats or peat pots using disease-free starting soil, and cover with ½ inch of vermiculite or milled sphagnum moss. Water thoroughly and place in plastic bags or under glass. Since most seeds require darkness for germination, cover containers with cardboard or newspaper.

Once seedlings have been hardened-off in the cold frame, set out in the garden in rows 24 to 30 inches apart, with about 15 to 24 inches between plants. Press soil firmly around roots to eliminate air pockets, and discourage cutworms by placing cardboard collars around stems. Water generously and protect from high winds or glaring sun for the first few days, if necessary.

CULTURE: Weeds, disease, and insects are perennial enemies of eggplant. Weeds can be removed with the shallow cultivations of the hoe. Disease can best be avoided by planting in an area of the garden that has not produced tomatoes, potatoes, or other eggplant within the last three years. And insects may be removed by hand, or combated with a spray compounded for use in the vegetable garden. Good ventilation is one of the best defenses against fungus and blights.

HARVEST: Eggplant fruits will be ready for picking when about 4 inches in diameter, although smaller fruits can be taken to the dinner table. Be sure to pick fruits while their skin is glossy; once the shine fades, they begin to deteriorate. Since vines will continue to blossom and set fruit regardless of impending frost, it's best to pinch off new blossoms as they appear. This will encourage the plants to produce a handful of good fruit, rather than an abundance of inferior fruit.

ENDIVE

Endive's resistance to cooler temperatures and even frost makes it a favorite of lettuce-lovers who crave tender greens long after the lettuce season. It also flourishes during the warmer months when lettuce bolts to seed and becomes bitter and unusable.

VARIETIES: Two types of endive are available: the broad-leaved, often referred to as escarole, and the curly-leaved, which is said to be more tender. The best-known of the broad-leaved types is Broad Leaved Batavian, but Florida Deep Heart is equally reliable. Of the curly-leaved types, Green Curled is most often recommended.

PLANTING: Endive will thrive wherever lettuce can be grown. If soil is "quick"—that is, warms very quickly in the spring—all the better for an early crop. Some gardeners like to begin the season with lettuce and plant endive as a fall crop in the space made available after peas, beans, or carrots have been harvested. Sow seeds in furrows no deeper than ¼ inch, and space rows 18 to 24 inches apart. Plan on succession-plantings, or start seeds indoors in order to transplant seedlings to the garden.

CULTURE: Once seedlings have emerged and become established, thin plants to stand 6 inches apart. Thinnings can be transplanted to another section of the garden or taken to the dinner table. Thin again to 12 inches apart. To ensure an abundance of tender leaves, feed plants at weekly intervals (if you use a once-a-season fertilizer, this extra feeding is not necessary). A mulch will help retain soil moisture and keep plants clean.

HARVEST: Both the broad-leaved and curly-leaved endive must be blanched in order to produce creamy white centers and to prevent leaves from becoming tough and bitter. When plants have reached maturity, simply gather outer leaves over the top of the plant and secure with rubber bands or string. Another method is to place a wide board directly on top of plants to block out sunlight. Be sure to remove the board after rainfalls to prevent rotting of plants.

G

GROUND CHERRY

Sometimes called husk or strawberry tomato, the ground cherry produces unique, dwarf,

lantern-like flowers that contain a small berry-like fruit. Ground cherries can be eaten raw, or dried for later use.

VARIETIES: Available mostly from specialty seedsmen, ground cherry may be listed under other names such as Chinese lantern plant, or cape or dwarf gooseberry.

PLANTING: A tender annual, ground cherry should be planted after all danger of frost has passed. Considerable time can be gained by starting the seeds indoors, then transplanting seedlings after hardening-off in a cold frame or on the back porch. Plants ought to stand 1 to 2 feet apart in rows 15 to 24 inches apart.

CULTURE: Protect freshly planted seedlings from intense sun, and keep soil from drying out. Remove weeds as they appear. Plants tend to sprawl, and may self-sow.

HARVEST: Pick husks when ripe. They may be eaten immediately or dried in the sun for later use.

H

HORSERADISH

Horseradish, grown for its white, parsnip-shaped roots, makes a coveted condiment when ground and mixed with white vinegar. Served with meats and fish, horseradish has a distinct, pungent flavor many people enjoy.

VARIETIES: Most seed suppliers offer the standard variety, known as Maliner Kren.

PLANTING: Although it is a perennial, most growers treat

tubers much like the white potato, and in fact, is often grown as a substitute for potatoes. It does not do well in extreme heat.

VARIETIES: Artichoke tubers may be obtained from a reliable supplier of vegetable seeds.

PLANTING: As soon as the ground can be worked, plant tubers in rows 3 to 4 feet apart; space individual plants about 18 to 24 inches apart. It's best to cover tubers with at least 4 inches of soil. Requiring a long season, the Jerusalem artichoke is a heavy feeder and will respond well to applications of a complete fertilizer or organic materials.

CULTURE: Weeds should not be allowed to encroach upon young plants. Once matured, however, the plants will keep weeds in check by casting a dense shade. To aid tuber development, some growers remove flowers as soon as they appear.

HARVEST: In the fall, dig roots with a spading fork, or allow them to winter-over under a mulch. Stalks should be cut to the ground to facilitate digging. The thin-skinned tubers keep well for several months in fairly dry storage at a temperature at or near 32 degrees F.

K

KALE

The deeply crinkled leaves of kale, subtly infused with delightful shades of blue, make it a natural for ornamental purposes. For gardeners who want to combine the practical with the aesthetic, kale is a must.

VARIETIES: Among the top varieties are Vates or Dwarf Blue Curled, and Dwarf Siberian.

PLANTING: A non-heading type of cabbage, kale calls for similar culture. Any good garden soil with

horseradish as an annual; that is, they sow sets in the spring for a fall harvest. It's also possible to set out horseradish in the fall to winter-over for a spring harvest. In either case, horseradish clearly prefers cooler temperatures. Purchase sets from a reliable supplier and plant as soon as the soil can be worked. Try to prepare soil to a depth of 8 inches, and remove as many clumps and roots as possible. If manure is used, work it in to an even deeper depth. Place sets 12 inches apart, being sure to keep the thicker end higher than the bottom end. Cover with 4 to 6 inches of soil. Rows should be spaced at least 2 feet apart.

CULTURE: Once shoots have broken through, plants should be kept free of invading weeds. After hand-picking weeds, hoe lightly along each side of the row, being careful to cultivate top of soil only. Supplementary applications of a high-potassium fertilizer at 10- to 14-day intervals will boost root and top growth.

HARVEST: Mature roots can be dug in the fall, or plants may be wintered-over by protecting roots with mulch.

J

JERUSALEM ARTICHOKE

Adaptable to a wide range of soils, the Jerusalem artichoke develops

adequate drainage will do. Because it is hardy and, in fact, improves in flavor after a mild frost, kale can be grown at either end of the growing season. Sow seed in shallow furrows as soon as the soil can be worked. Taller varieties may be started indoors, but low-growing types do not transplant well and should be sown where they will stand in the garden. Rows can be spaced as close as 18 inches apart or up to 30 inches apart, depending on the variety and whether the garden is to be machine- or hand-cultivated.

CULTURE: Although kale is an easy crop to grow, it pays to encourage rapid growth by providing plenty of nutrients and moisture. If hot, dry weather threatens, spread a mulch around plants to keep root systems cool and moist.

HARVEST: Kale will supply a continuous crop if outer leaves are picked as they mature. Or, entire plants can be pulled. To extend harvest, cover plants with mulch as protection against severe frost. Kale can be wintered-over if given sufficient protection.

KOHLRABI

Kohlrabi has the peculiar habit of producing beet-shaped knobs that grow just above the soil level. The cabbage-like leaves sprout from the knob, and both leaf stems and the enlarged root stalk are edible.

VARIETIES: Reliable varieties include Early White Vienna and Early Burpee Vienna.

PLANTING: A member of the

cabbage family, kohlrabi also prefers cooler temperatures, and plenty of sun. Once ground has become manageable, plant seed ½ inch deep in rows 24 inches apart. For an even earlier crop, sow seed indoors about six to eight weeks before the average date of last frost. Harden-off young seedlings in a cold frame or on the back porch before planting in the garden. Plants should stand about 4 to 6 inches apart. Try to shift the annual location of plants belonging to the brassica group to prevent disease attacks.

CULTURE: When planted from seed in the spring (or midsummer for a fall crop), seedlings should be thinned to prevent crowding. Thin the first time to 3 inches between plants, and finally to 6 inches between plants. Like cabbage, cauliflower, and broccoli, kohlrabi likes cooler temperatures and plenty of moisture. They also should be sprayed at weekly intervals with *Bacillus thuringiensis* to combat cabbage worms. Water frequently. A mulch will help maintain lower soil temperatures as well as preserve soil moisture. Cultivate lightly to avoid injuring surface roots, and try not to cover knobs with soil.
HARVEST: Kohlrabi will become tough and stringy if allowed to ripen beyond peak maturity. Pick before knobs grow greater than 2½ to 3 inches in diameter. Simply cut the knob from the main root at soil level. Older roots can still be used sliced raw in fresh salads.

L

LEEK

For subtlety of flavor, few things come close to the delicate taste of leeks. A favorite of gourmet cooks who take special delight in putting together enough leeks to make vichyssoise, leeks are a long-season crop and require a little extra planning by the home gardener.
VARIETIES: Among the best varieties is Conqueror, which is extra-hardy and therefore the perfect choice for wintering-over. Tivia is recommended for fall crops, while Broad London, known for its sweet and delicate flavor, is good for early spring planting.
PLANTING: Because seed is slow to grow, most gardeners start seed indoors in flats about eight weeks before the normal outside planting time. Leeks, like their cousin, the onion, need a neutral to slightly alkaline soil to do well. If you suspect excessive acidity, apply ground dolomitic limestone at the rate of 5 pounds per 100 square feet of garden area. If more is needed, apply in two doses at either end of the growing season. When transplanting seedlings, set into a depressed furrow about 5 to 6 inches below the soil line. As plants mature, gather soil against stems. This blanching procedure will produce tender, white stalks.

When planting from seed, sow at a depth of ½ inch and cover with sifted soil. When plants have reached a height of 8 inches, cut off half the tops and plant 5 inches apart in another row. Rows should

be 24 inches apart. Leeks appreciate a moist, nutrient-rich soil, so work in compost or rotted manure, being sure to remove all clumps and other debris from the area.
CULTURE: Because of their slender leaf stalks, leeks are practically defenseless against marauding weeds. Keep young seedlings protected by hand-picking weeds. Later, a mulch can be applied to hold in soil moisture and smother emerging weeds. If rainfall is scarce, sprinkle crop until watering is equivalent to 1 inch of rain per week. When plants are ready for blanching, pull back mulch and bank soil against stalks.
HARVEST: Resembling oversized scallions, leeks are ready for pulling when the stems are between 1 and 2½ inches across. If desired, leeks can be left in the garden to winter-over if given at least 6 to 8 inches of mulch protection.

LETTUCE

What could be more pedestrian than a simple leaf? Yet chances are, lettuce—grown exclusively for its tender leaves—can be found in more gardens than any other vegetable or herb.
VARIETIES: There are three types of lettuce: the loose-leaf variety, whose leaves can be picked as they mature; head lettuce; and the Cos type or upright lettuce. All have their devotees, although loose-leaf has a slight edge in popularity because it's easier to grow and provides a

continuous crop of leaves. Among the loose-leaf varieties are Black-Seeded Simpson, Buttercrunch, Oak Leaf, and Salad Bowl. The most popular heading types include Great Lakes, Burpee's Iceberg, and Dark Green Boston. Some upright favorites are Cos, Romaine, and Paris White.

PLANTING: The number of ways lettuce can be adapted to the garden is limited only by your imagination. Not only is lettuce resistant to frost, but it is a short-season crop, requiring from 50 to 80 days to mature. The trick is to arrange your garden space and planting schedule in such a way that fresh greens are ever-present on the dinner table. To get a jump on the outdoor growing season, start seeds indoors for transplanting in early spring. As soon as the ground can be prepared, transplant seedlings or sow directly from seed, leaving room for succession plantings spaced two or three weeks apart. Sow seed in shallow furrows. Since seed is light, pour a small amount into one hand and grip between forefinger and thumb of the other hand. Cover with no more than ¼ inch of soil, and sprinkle with water.

An excellent way to get the most from your garden space is to squeeze the lettuce patch in between rows of slower-growing crops such as cabbage, cauliflower, or broccoli. Or, incorporate the crinkle-leaved, decorative varieties into your landscaping plans.

CULTURE: Because lettuce seed is small, the row likely will be overcrowded so thinnings will be necessary. When seedlings are about 4 inches high, thin to 3 inches apart. Thinnings can be eaten or transplanted in another section of the garden. Later, thin to 6 inches apart, and finally, to 12 to 18 inches. To encourage leafy growth, fertilize with a high-nitrogen fertilizer, keeping it well away from leaves.

When cultivating with the hoe, avoid getting soil on or against plants. The idea is to produce high-quality leaves.

Warm weather will cause lettuce to bolt; plants will send up long stems topped with seed stalks. Some varieties such as Slobolt are resistant to higher temperatures and

may be more suited to midsummer plantings. If plants appear to be suffering from heat, help reduce temperatures by mulching plants and providing partial shade.

HARVEST: The loose-leaf varieties are the darlings of the lettuce family because their outer leaves can be picked as they mature, leaving the inner leaves for later pickings. The heading types allow only one picking, since the complete plants are harvested. To pick leaves, simply pinch them off at the base of the plant. Heads are removed by cutting the stem at soil level.

M

MUSKMELON

Planting muskmelon (or cantaloupe) involves a small risk, since conditions alone can spell the difference between success and failure. But a good crop of sweet, vine-ripened melons is so enjoyable that memories of old failures will quickly vanish.

VARIETIES: Among the most reliable varieties are Burpee Hybrid, Ambrosia, Delicious 51, Iroquois, and Samson Hybrid.

PLANTING: Muskmelon demands not only a long growing season, but also plenty of warm days and nights, moisture, and adequate nutrients. After all danger of frost has passed and the soil has thoroughly warmed, plant seeds, five to a hill, ¾ to 1 inch deep. Hills should be spaced 4 to 6 feet apart, with rows 6 to 8 feet apart. For a nutritional boost, place several shovelfuls of rotted manure or compost beneath each hill. Cover with a 4-inch layer of soil, plant seed, and moisten each hill thoroughly. In areas where nights may get chilly, a black plastic mulch will go a long way toward keeping soil temperatures from dropping. At the same time, weeds will be eliminated and moisture retained.

CULTURE: Once melon seedlings have developed a third set of true leaves, thin out weaker plants to allow three plants per hill. Make certain young plants are not deprived of moisture. Weed periodically, but take care not to disturb tender root structures. When fruits begin to appear, place a board or a square of shingle or roofing paper under fruits to hasten ripening and prevent rot.

HARVEST: As melons become larger, the temptation is great to pick fruits prematurely. A ripe melon will not only have an irresistible odor, but also will slip easily from its stem. If any tugging is required, leave the melon to ripen a little longer.

MUSTARD

Grown primarily in southern regions, mustard is grown for its abundance of succulent leaves. In northern gardens, cool-resistant mustard can be sown as an early spring or fall leaf crop.

VARIETIES: Like endive, mustard offers both the curly- and broad-leaved varieties. Among the better-known curly types are Burpee's Fordhook and Southern Giant Curled. Broad-leaved varieties include Florida Broad Leaf and the flavorful Tendergreen.

PLANTING: Because mustard runs quickly to seed, plantings should be scheduled for the cooler portions of the season—the winter months in the South, and early spring and fall in northern areas. Some vegetable growers like to start seed in the fall and winter-over young plants by insulating with generous layerings of mulch. When spring arrives, the mulch is pulled back and plants are allowed to revive. Sow seeds ½ inch deep in rows 18 to 20 inches apart.

Mature plants should stand at least 6 to 8 inches apart in the row.

CULTURE: Like all greens, mustard responds well to periodic applications of a nitrogen-rich fertilizer, either in the form of a commercial preparation or an organic source such as compost, fish scraps, or blood meal. Clean culture is especially important, since mustard has a tendency to ramble into other sections of the garden. Weed and thin regularly, and pinch off flower stems as soon as they appear to prevent plants from going to seed.

HARVEST: As plants develop, outer leaves can be picked. Or pull entire plants at peak maturity.

OKRA

Often the main ingredient of gumbo soup, okra is grown mainly in the South. The elongated, bean-like pods are picked and used in soups, or cooked and served as a vegetable.

VARIETIES: The chief varieties are Clemson Spineless, Dwarf Green Long Pod, and Emerald.

PLANTING: Because okra is extremely sensitive to unseasonable weather, it makes better sense to start seeds indoors a month and a half to two months before the last day of expected frost. Sow in flats or peat pots, then harden-off in a cold frame before transplanting to the garden. When sowing directly in the soil, plant in rows about 30 inches apart. Soil should be thoroughly prepared and rich in plant nutrients.

CULTURE: Thin young but established plants to stand about 6 inches apart. Thin again to a distance of 12 to 24 inches apart. Occasional side-dressings of fertilizer will encourage good growth. To combat weeds and hold in moisture, spread a mulch around the plants.

HARVEST: Pods are ready for picking when they are anywhere between 2½ and 7 inches long. The smaller the pod, the more tender it will be. Once plants have flowered and pods begun to form, pick daily to encourage peak production. When pods begin ripening, plants will no longer produce new pods.

ONIONS

For some home growers, a garden wouldn't be a garden if it didn't include an onion patch. Easy to grow, the onion comes in a seemingly unending array of colors, shapes, and sizes. There are white onions, purple onions, and yellow onions, in both bunching and single-bulb varieties.

VARIETIES: Among the numerous varieties, some favorite onion varieties are: Bunching: Southport White Bunching, and Evergreen Long White Bunching. Table onions include: Red Hamburger, Sweet Spanish, and Yellow Burmuda. Good winter storage onions are: Early Yellow Globe, White Portugal, Danvers Yellow Globe, and Ebenezer.

PLANTING: For a bountiful onion crop, the soil must be brimming with nutrients and constantly supplied with moisture. Since onions require anywhere from 100 to 120 days from the time seed is sown until mature bulbs can be pulled, most gardeners buy small sets (about the size of a dime) from a garden supply center. The sets can be planted 1 inch deep and about 4 inches apart as soon as the soil can be worked. Be sure the pointed end of the set is facing up so leaves can grow unhindered. Cover with soil and tamp gently to remove air pockets. Early greens can be enjoyed by planting sets every 2 inches instead of 4, and then pulling every other plant when it comes time to thin the row.

It's also possible to launch the onion patch by transplanting seedling plants which may be ordered from a reliable seedsman or purchased wherever gardening supplies are sold. Place seedlings 3 or 4 inches apart along the furrow and about 1 inch deep. Firm soil around roots and sprinkle with water so soil settles firmly against plants.

Some home growers like to plant onions from seed not only because of the greater challenge, but also because seeds are much cheaper. You also can get a better selection of varieties if you start your crop from seed. Sow seed as early in spring as possible in rows ½ inch deep and 12 to 24 inches apart, depending on whether you plan to hand- or machine-cultivate. You can plant closer, if you mulch instead of cultivate. Seed on the thick side to ensure a respectable crop, and since seeds are slow to germinate, be sure to mix in some radish seeds to help mark the row. Thinnings make delicious additions to salads.

CULTURE: Many vegetables, especially the vine crops, manage their own defenses against weeds by developing wide, broad leaves. Weeds, unable to get sufficient sunshine, soon wither and die. Onions, on the other hand, produce slender, tubular stalks that cast very little shadow. In no time, the row can disappear beneath a forest of weeds. The best time to nip a weed is when it first becomes visible. Pull by hand where they grow among plants, then use a hoe to eliminate weeds between rows. Side-dressings of fertilizer and frequent waterings will help plants along. Mulches are useful when growing onions.

HARVEST: Toward late summer, the tops will begin to brown and some will flop over. When about three-quarters of the tops have fallen, knock the remaining stalks to the ground with a rake or stiff broom. Pull bulbs when stalks are completely brown, and spread them out on the ground for a few days to cure in the sun. To store, cut off stems about 1 inch from the bulb and place in slatted boxes or open mesh containers. Or, weave the dried stems together to make an "onion rope" and hang in a cool, dark place. Most storage onions will last three months or more.

P

PARSNIP

Parsnips are a long-time favorite for adding a delicate, sweet flavor to stews or soups. They can even take the sting out of winter by offering a taste of summer while snow still covers the ground: dig up the roots as winter is ebbing for a delicious garden treat at a time when most gardeners are wondering when to order seeds.

VARIETIES: The traditional varieties include Hollow Crown and Harris' Model.

PLANTING: The soil for parsnips must be worked thoroughly, since the edible root portion may grow as deep as 15 inches. Rake and remove all stones and other debris which might obstruct the normal development of roots. Sow seeds thickly in rows 18 to 24 inches apart. Since seed germinates slowly, a handful of radish seed should be mixed with the parsnip seed as a means of marking the row. If soil tends to crust, cover seed with milled sphagnum moss or peat moss mixed with soil. Water thoroughly. A light mulch of dried grass clippings will help retain soil moisture.

CULTURE: Once the carrot-like tops have pushed through the soil, invading weeds should be removed. When plants are 4 to 6 inches high, thin to 6 inches apart. A second thinning is necessary to provide at least 8 inches of space between mature plants.

HARVEST: Parsnips are one of the few vegetable crops that actually improve in flavor after being nipped by frost. But mature roots should be dug before the ground freezes. Try wintering-over a half of a row by covering it with a straw mulch. Then, when spring seems just around the corner, pull back the mulch and dig roots as needed.

PEAS

One of the most rewarding sights in any vegetable garden is the pea patch in full bloom. Graceful vines and clouds of delicate white blossoms make the plants unusually ornamental. A cool-season crop, peas do well with just a handful of rich soil, a reasonable supply of moisture, and cool temperatures.

VARIETIES: Part of the joy of growing peas is the variety of uses to which they can be put. Certain types, such as the edible-podded or sugar peas, may be grown just for their tender, flavorful pods. Varieties of edible-podded peas include Oregon Sugar Pod, Mammoth Melting Sugar, and Dwarf Gray Sugar. There are also early peas, such as Alaska (55 days) and Little Marvel (62 days). Of the sweet pea varieties, the most notable are Sparkle, Wando, Freezonian, Progress No. 9, Alderman, and Green Arrow.

PLANTING: Peas will sag, yellow, and do poorly in warm weather, so be sure to plan pea plantings for the early part of the growing season. Sow seeds as soon as the soil can be put into shape in the spring. Usually, peas are planted in double rows with fencing or netting placed in between as support. Some gardeners prefer wide-row planting, which calls for an 8-inch-wide furrow. In either case, the seed should be planted about 1 to 2 inches deep in rows spaced 24 to 30 inches apart. Plants should be allowed to stand 2 to 3 inches apart in the row; as a rule, thinning is not necessary. Peas are legumes, which means that their roots develop small nodules that are capable of producing extra amounts of nitrogen. To aid formation of these nodules, gardeners often innoculate seed before planting. Simply mix innoculating powder, available at most garden supply centers, with seed that has been lightly sprinkled with water.

CULTURE: When the plants are between 3 and 4 inches high, begin light supplementary feedings of commercial fertilizer at 10- to 14-day intervals. Be sure granules do not come in direct contact with tender stems, roots, or leaves, and avoid over-fertilizing, which can cause vines to spend more time producing leaves than blossoms and pods. As soon as weeds appear, cultivate with a hoe, but keep the blade from penetrating too deeply in order to preserve moisture and avoid injuring roots. If warm, dry weather arrives earlier than expected, cool conditions can be approximated by the use of mulching material.

HARVEST: A careful eye should be kept on the vines as harvest time approaches to prevent pods from becoming overripe. Outer skins of pods should feel firm but not too hard to the touch. Overripe peas will crack and taste mealy. As soon as ripening starts, the pea patch should be checked each day. Use spent pea vines as an excellent mulch around late maturing sweet corn.

PEANUT

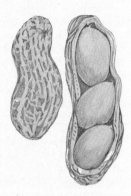

In terms of growth habits, few crops are as intricate and as intriguing as the peanut. After flowering, the stalks work their way into the soil where the shells and "peas" develop. Grown mostly in southern regions, peanuts prefer a light soil.
VARIETIES: Best-known because of its small, sweet nuts is the Spanish variety. Jumbo Virginia peanuts produce extra-sized nuts in 120 days.
PLANTING: Before planting peanuts, the soil should be worked thoroughly until it is as friable as possible. Since peanuts require a "sweet" or alkaline soil, it's important to incorporate ground dolomitic limestone into the garden whenever needed. Manure, compost, or commercial fertilizer are excellent materials for maintaining necessary nutrient levels. Once all danger of frost has passed and the soil has warmed, plant seeds either with or without shells 4 to 6 inches apart and 2 inches deep. Rows should be spaced at least 2 feet apart.
CULTURE: Once seedlings have emerged and become established, thin to stand between 8 and 12 inches apart in the row. Weeds should be kept from invading the growing plants.
HARVEST: Well before frost in the fall, dig plants; gently shake loose soil from roots and allow to dry before removing peanut pods. Store peanut pods in airtight jars.

PEPPERS

Most cooks would feel severely restricted, if not helpless, without the flavor-packed pepper. Although somewhat temperamental because of its extreme sensitivity to unfavorable conditions, peppers still deserve a spot in every garden.
VARIETIES: Peppers fall into two groups: sweet and hot. The common market variety is simply a sweet pepper that has been harvested before ripening to a bright red color. Hot peppers, as the name suggests, possess a pungent, spicy flavor. Popular sweet pepper varieties include Canape, California Wonder, Yolo Wonder, and Bell Boy Hybrid. Hot Portugal, Large Cherry, and Long Red Cayenne are reliable hot pepper varieties.
PLANTING: In order for peppers to blossom and set fruit without mishap, anywhere from 60 to 80 days of consistently warm days and nights are required. The plants will thrive in just about any soil as long as drainage is good. In northern regions where the growing season is shorter, most gardeners start seeds indoors in flats or peat pots 6 to 8 weeks before their frost-free date. After seedlings have been hardened-off in the cold frame, transplant them to the garden. Allow 18 to 24 inches between plants and 20 to 36 inches between rows. Cutworms may be a nuisance, so plant stems should be protected with a collar of stiff cardboard or aluminum foil. Be sure the collar is inserted at least ½ inch into the soil. When watering transplants, use lukewarm water to avoid root shock caused by cold tap water.

CULTURE: Pepper is one of those crops that responds so well to fertilizer that it will spend all of its time producing stems and leaves instead of fruit. Therefore, go easy on fertilizer, especially nitrogen-rich supplements. Also, keep weeds from crowding plants and competing for soil nutrients. If blossoms drop off and fruits do not set, be patient; given warmer conditions, the plants will blossom a second time and produce a healthy crop of fruit.
HARVEST: Since green pepper is just an immature red pepper, you can pick and use peppers at any stage of their development. For somewhat sweeter-tasting red peppers, wait until fruit turns color before harvesting.

POTATO

For some, the appearance of spuds on the dinner table means hard times. But new potatoes freshly dug from the garden have a delicacy of flavor that makes them more than respectable. Potatoes require a little more in the way of growing room and are sometimes more susceptible to bugs and disease than are other crops. But even a single row is enough to provide a treat for the whole family.
VARIETIES: For early-maturing potatoes, try Irish Cobbler or Norland. Good longer-season types are Katahdin and Kennebec.
PLANTING: The most important requirement for growing potatoes is a soil acidic enough to discourage the development of "scab" disease, which renders the tubers unsightly and also affects their storage life. The best way to fertilize is by placing a band of complete fertilizer beneath the furrow and covering with soil. Use about 7 pounds per 100 feet of row, and cover with at least 3 inches of soil. Although some growers cut up market potatoes that have begun

to sprout, it makes better sense to purchase standard "seed" potatoes that have been processed for that purpose. Slice potatoes into sections in such a way that each has one or two "eyes" or sprouts. Set in the furrow and cover with 4 to 6 inches of soil. A cool-season vegetable, potatoes can be sown early in the spring as long as the soil is not too wet.

CULTURE: As soon as the young vines begin to spread, cultivate out weeds, taking care not to injure growing root systems. As tubers begin to form, it helps to bank soil against plants to prevent sunlight from striking the potatoes. If exposed to sunlight for too long, the skins will turn green and the tubers will become inedible.

HARVEST: As the season comes to a close, the vines will gradually wither and turn brown. When vines have died back completely, dig tubers with a garden spade. If you plan to squirrel away a sack or two for winter use, take extra care not to damage potatoes. Choose a sunny, dry day for digging, since the tubers are difficult to remove from wet, soggy soil.

PUMPKIN

Not many people are so blessed with garden space that they can enjoy the luxury of pumpkins, which, because of their size and rambling habits, require more room than any other vegetable. Yet, with a little clever planning, almost everyone can squeeze at least one vine into their patio or homestead garden.

VARIETIES: Pumpkins are available in all sizes, from the gargantuan jack-o'-lantern varieties to the small sweet-fleshed types grown for cooking purposes. There are even several naked-seed varieties like Triple Treat and Lady Godiva, for devotees of dried pumpkin seeds. Standard large varieties are Big Max, Big Tom, and Howden's Field. Intermediate-sized varieties include Jackpot and Spirit Hybrid. Smaller fruits are produced from Small Sugar and Spookie. A recent development is Cinderella, a bush variety which requires less space.

PLANTING: Pumpkins do best when neither too cold nor too hot. After danger of frost has passed and the ground is good and warm, gather soil into hills 4 to 6 feet apart with rows separated by 6 to 8 feet. Sow four to five seeds per hill. When plants are well-rooted, thin out weaker plants, leaving at least three per hill. If space is a problem, let vines climb a sunny fence, or plant them next to corn where they can use spent stalks for support. If a fence is not handy, build a portable trellis for vertical growth.

CULTURE: Once vines have begun to sprawl and leaves to form, weeds will have little chance because of the dense shade. But seedling plants should be kept free of weed competitors. A mulch is useful for weed control and also helps keep fruits clean.

HARVEST: Leave pumpkins on the vine until the threat of frost nears. Then cut stems, leaving a portion (about 2 inches) on the fruit, and allow to "cure" in the sun a few days. If frost seems likely, cure in a shed or on a porch.

R

RADISH

Small and broadleaved, the radish is barely distinguishable from a weed. Yet, more often than not, the first seed a beginning gardener plants is a radish seed. Easy to grow and very quick to sprout, radishes thrive virtually anywhere, from patio tub to between lettuce plants.

VARIETIES: Radish varieties are generally grouped according to their shape or color. Some are red, others white, while still others are black or a combination of red and white. Icicle radishes have carrot-like roots up to 5 inches in length. Popular red varieties are Cherry Belle, Red Boy, Scarlet Globe, and Champion. White varieties include Icicle, Burpee White, and Summer Cross. Sparkler develops globe-shaped roots that are half red and white. Round Black Spanish and Celestial are winter varieties ideal for late-summer and fall planting.

PLANTING: The secret to juicy, tender radishes is rapid growth. In hot, dry weather, roots will limp along and most likely become hard and bitter. Sow seed as early as possible in rich, well-prepared soil, and be sure plants are given ample moisture. Seed can be planted ¾ inch deep in rows 12 inches apart. A light mulch will help keep weeds down and prevent the soil from baking. Radishes are a natural for space-saving techniques and will do nicely as a border plant or between rows of larger vegetables. It's wise to make room for a number of succession-plantings in order to enjoy a continuous supply.

CULTURE: Once plants have broken through the soil, thin to stand at least 2 inches apart. Remember, nothing is gained by overcrowding, since globes will be at best misshapen, and at worst, too skinny to be of any use. Keep moist and well-fertilized to ensure rapid and continuous growth.

HARVEST: A split radish is most likely an overripe radish. Be sure to check root tops periodically as maturation nears, and don't be lured into thinking the larger the radish, the better.

RHUBARB

For the gardener who hopes to refine the art of growing until the most can be grown with the least expenditure of effort, rhubarb is a must. Easy to grow, rhubarb pokes through season after season for years of effort-free harvests. All that is required beyond initial planting is an occasional dose of nutrient-rich compost or rotted manure.

VARIETIES: The standard varieties of rhubarb include MacDonald, Valentine, and Victoria.

PLANTING: In order to reap the rewards of rhubarb sooner, most gardeners start their rhubarb patch from roots available at a garden supply center or from a reliable seedsman. Starting from seed is possible, but it takes two years for the plants to become sufficiently established for picking. Plants grown from root stocks, on the other hand, will withstand moderate pickings after the first year. Rhubarb does best in a thoroughly prepared soil that is well-stocked with an abundance of plant nutrients. Work the soil to at least a depth of 10 inches and incorporate generous amounts of compost or well-rotted manure. Plant roots 4 to 6 inches deep and about 4 feet apart. Be sure to locate the rhubarb patch to one side of the garden where it can thrive unmolested by machinery.

CULTURE: During the first year, keep weeds under control by periodic hand-picking. If possible, use a mulching material to smother weeds and keep moisture in the soil. Compost or manure are excellent mulches because they supply a smattering of nutrients as well.

Once plants have become established, they will invariably develop a long flower stalk that should be promptly removed in order to channel all growth into stalks and leaves. Eventually, after seven to eight years, the plants will become thick and overgrown, causing the stalks to become more and more spindly. This is the time to split roots for new plantings. Each root division should have at least three leaf buds, as well as a healthy section of root. Plant at 4-foot intervals in another section of the garden, and water thoroughly. Divisions may be made in early spring or in the fall.

HARVEST: Rhubarb is one of the earliest plants to poke deep-green leaf buds through what looks like a lifeless soil. Once stalks have matured, grasp them at base of plant and gently pull from the root crown with a slight twisting motion. During the first year, only a light picking should be attempted. By the second and third years, however, the plants will be fully established. At no time should you pick more than a third of the plant.

The leaves of the rhubarb plant contain oxalic acid and should never be used for food purposes. Remove leaves from harvested stalks and add them to the compost pile.

ROQUETTE

A quick-and-easy way to enjoy the flavor of horseradish is to cultivate a row or two of roquette. A salad plant grown in cool weather, roquette leaves are sometimes considered an herb. Their pungent, horseradish-like flavor is a delightful addition to mixed salads.

PLANTING: Roquette prefers a rich, moist soil containing ample amounts of plant nutrients. Plant seed in shallow furrows separating rows by at least 1 foot. Plants should stand 3 to 4 inches apart. For a continuous crop, succession-sow at two- or three-week intervals.

CULTURE: Rapid growth is essential, which means that the soil should not be allowed to dry out. If an unexpected drought occurs, mulch plants with a 4- to 6-inch layer of straw, dried lawn clippings, or half-rotted compost.

HARVEST: Pick leaves as they develop. Since older leaves can be tough and on the strong side, the younger the leaf, the better.

RUTABAGA AND TURNIP

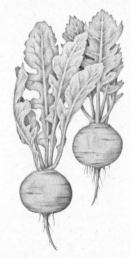

Because they're tolerant to cool weather, turnips and rutabagas are excellent for planting in spaces where earlier crops—such as peas, beets, carrots, and spinach—have come and gone. Sometimes referred to as the Swedish turnip or Canadian turnip, rutabagas are often preferred for their richer flavor. Culture is similar for both.

VARIETIES: The most reliable turnip varieties include Tokyo

Market, Foliage or Shogoin (grown also for greens), Just Right, and Purple Top White Globe. Rutabaga varieties are restricted primarily to Macomber and Purple Top.

PLANTING: Both turnips and rutabagas may be planted in early spring, but most home growers sow them in midsummer in order to enjoy a fall crop and to provide enough roots for winter storage. A well-prepared soil, free of obstructions, will contribute to healthy, well-formed roots. Work in a 5-10-10 or a vegetable-garden fertilizer unless ample nutrients were incorporated for the previous crop. In most cases, enough will be available to sustain a second growth. Plant seeds about ½ inch deep and cover with soil mixed with sand and peat moss. Since seeds are slow to germinate, include a dash of rapidly germinating radish seed to mark the row. Rutabaga seeds may be planted somewhat deeper.

CULTURE: Using the emerging radish seedlings as a guide, remove weeds as soon as they threaten to engulf the row. After plants have grown to a height of 4 to 6 inches, thin turnips to 4 to 6 inches, and rutabagas to 6 to 9 inches between plants. A mulch can be a valuable aid in keeping weeds at a minimum and preserving soil moisture.

HARVEST: Turnips should be dug before hard frosts threaten roots. Try to harvest on the young side, since overripe turnips can be coarse and bitter. The tops of roots should measure anywhere from 2 to 3 inches in diameter. Rutabagas, on the other hand, may be dug after frost or left in the ground protected by a thick 6- to 8-inch layer of straw or leaf mulch.

S

SALSIFY

Closely resembling a turnip and grown in the same way as parsnips and rutabagas, salsify is coveted for the subtle oyster-like flavor of its roots. Hence, it is sometimes referred to as oyster plant.

VARIETIES: The standard variety, available from most seed

distributors, and nurseries, is Sandwich Island Mammoth.

PLANTING: Salsify requires an extended growing season numbering at least 100 days, and a well-prepared, rich soil. If manure is applied, be certain that it's well-rotted and doesn't contain clumps and other debris that may cause roots to fork and become misshapen. Sow seed as early as the soil will permit, about ½ inch deep in rows spaced 16 to 24 inches apart.

CULTURE: Weed out rows periodically until salsify leaves are dense enough to offer some self-protection. Thereafter, cultivate gently between rows with a hoe, or spread a 4-inch layer of mulching material around plants. Thin to stand 3 to 6 inches apart in the row.

HARVEST: Somewhat thinner than the parsnip root, salsify can be pulled whenever they have reached a desirable size. The mature root is no more than 1 to 1½ inches in diameter at the crown, and may grow as long as 7 to 10 inches. With adequate protection, the roots may be left in the ground over winter for a spring harvest.

SHALLOT

A member of the onion family, shallots possess a delightfully mild flavor that is especially delicious when added to soups or stews. The greens also may be used.

PLANTING: Shallots are planted in much the same way as garlic and onion. Small bulbs or cloves are set out as early in spring as possible or,

in southern regions, in fall for a winter harvest. The soil should be well-drained and supplied with nutrients. Set bulbs about 1 inch deep and between 2 and 3 inches apart. Cover with soil and tamp lightly. Try to keep the point barely below or just breaking through the soil surface.

CULTURE: Protect young sprouts from weeds, and hoe between rows, being careful not to disturb shallow root systems.

HARVEST: As picking time approaches, the tops will gradually die back in much the same way as onions. Flatten remaining stalks and pull bulbs when they have turned brown. Dry and store as for onions.

SPINACH

Because of its high vitamin content and exuberant growth, spinach could well be the king of the leaf crops. It is one of the easiest vegetables to grow, being highly resistant to frost and almost maintenance-free.

VARIETIES: A number of varieties are available, including some which are not strictly of the spinach family. Among the reliable varieties are

Viking, Winter Bloomsdale, and Melody Hybrid. New Zealand, which is not a true spinach, is resistant to warmer weather.

PLANTING: Spinach definitely prefers the cooler portions of the growing season, as well as a soil slightly on the "sweet" or alkaline side. A pH reaction of between 6.0 and 6.5 is best. If a soil test reveals an overly acid condition, work in appropriate amounts of agricultural lime at the rate of 5 pounds per 100 square feet of garden area. The richer and better-prepared the soil, the more abundant the crop will be. Because the leaves form the crop, any material high in nitrogen will contribute to rapid, succulent growth. Sow seeds as early as practical, ¾ inch deep in rows 14 to 18 inches apart. For a continuous crop, sow at ten-day intervals.

CULTURE: When young plants are 4 to 6 inches high, thin so plants stand 3 inches apart in the row. Removed plants may be eaten raw or cooked. This first thinning is a good time to apply a side dressing of nitrogen-rich fertilizer. The final thinning should allow 5 inches between plants. Keep weeds at a minimum, and mulch if material is handy, especially if hot weather threatens to slow growth.

HARVEST: Outer leaves of the plants may be picked as soon as they are ready, or the entire plant can be pulled. Spinach will tend to bolt to seed in hot weather, so harvesting should be completed before warmer temperatures arrive.

SQUASH

When it comes to size, shape, and color, nothing is quite as exotic and mind-boggling as the squash. Some are round, bulbous, and multi-colored, while others display various bumps, twists, and turns. There are smooth-skinned varieties such as zucchini and cocozelle. Most peculiar of all is spaghetti squash, whose tangled, stringy flesh is cooked and served in many delightful recipes. Some squash are extremely practical because they store well into winter, while others have few culinary uses and instead are displayed as colorful ornaments.

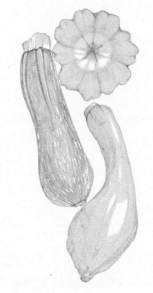

VARIETIES: Of the summer varieties, the most notable are Early Prolific Straightneck (yellow), zucchini Elite, Fordhook Zucchini, Cocozelle Bush (all green), White Bush Patty Pan, and Scallopini Hybrid. Fall and winter varieties include Royal Acorn, Table Queen, Waltham Butternut, Bush Butternut, Blue Hubbard, Buttercup, Bush Acorn, Table King, and Bush Gold Nugget.

PLANTING: Most squash grow on long, rambling vines that practically take over the garden. However, in recent years great strides have been made in developing bush varieties with much more compact growth habits. So if space is a factor, look for a bush variety. The soil should be warm and beyond all danger of frost before sowing squash seed. If the soil seems unusually damp, rake it into hills for better drainage. Plant four to five seeds per hill. Winter squash takes more room, so hills should be at least 6 to 8 feet apart. Summer squash hills can be spaced as close as 6 feet. Space all bush varieties 3 to 4 feet apart. In order to provide readily available nutrients, place a shovelful or two of manure under each hill, or work it thoroughly into the soil.

CULTURE: After seeds have sprouted and plants begun to form vines, thin hills to three healthy plants each. Weeds should be removed immediately, and the soil gently cultivated with a hoe. A mulch

can go a long way toward eliminating weeds and maintaining moisture in the soil.

HARVEST: Once summer squash blooms, the fruits develop with almost lightning speed. A watchful eye should be kept on the plants, since squash can easily become overripe. Pick summer varieties when young and tender. The skin should be soft and easy to pierce with your fingernail. Winter squash, on the other hand, must be allowed to fully mature on the vine so the rinds can become thick and hard. Cut stems, leaving 1 or 2 inches remaining on the fruit, and allow to cure by exposing to the sun for a day or two. If frost threatens, cure in a ventilated area, such as a shed, porch, or open garage.

SUNFLOWER

The versatile sunflower has so many advantages that it could well be called the "fun" flower. Kids will gawk in wonder at the huge, brilliant blossom that follows the sun across the sky, and grown-ups with a weakness for snacks will appreciate its delicious seeds. For bird lovers, the sunflower offers a cheap supply of food for the winter months.

VARIETIES: There are a number of sunflower varieties, but the one best-suited for food purposes is Mammoth.

PLANTING: In view of its jack-in-the-beanstalk size, it's no wonder the sunflower does best in rich, deeply dug soil that can supply the required amount of moisture. Plant seeds in permanent locations about ½ inch deep and about 1 foot apart. Because they are fairly hardy, they can be planted in early spring. It's also possible to start young plants indoors for transplanting after they have been hardened-off in a cold frame.

CULTURE: Once plants begin to reach an appreciable height, provide supports in the form of poles made from saplings or purchased at a garden supply center. Some support may be provided simply by hilling earth against the lower portion of the stalks. As flowers begin to fade, remove them immediately from the stalk to encourage additional blooms.

HARVEST: Allow flowers to fully ripen so seeds will have a chance to mature. Hang cut flower heads in a well-ventilated area. Seeds will separate easily when flowers are sufficiently dry.

SWEET POTATO

Once relegated to the commercial grower, sweet potatoes are gradually becoming more popular with home growers. This long-season crop is now commonly available as starts in the North during the spring. The main requirement for a bountiful harvest is a long growing season. If your frost-free growing period is 150 days or more, sweet potatoes are worth a try.

VARIETIES: Recommended varieties are Jersey Orange,

Nugget, Nemagold, Centennial, and Goldrush.

PLANTING: Soil conditions are critical to the proper formation of sweet potatoes. The ground must be thoroughly worked and decidedly loose; a compact, hard soil will cause tubers to become thin and stringy. A moderately fertile, sandy loam is ideal. If a commercial fertilizer is used, be sure to apply it sparingly and make sure granules are mixed thoroughly with the soil. Because of its slow growth, most growers start their plants in hotbeds (heated cold frames) well before the weather is warm enough to permit planting outdoors. Roots purchased from a garden supply center or reputable seedsman are planted close together in the hotbed and covered with 2 inches of sand or fine soil. As the plants grow, allow free air circulation by leaving the hotbed cover propped open. The slightly lower temperatures will acclimate plants to outdoor conditions. When the threat of frost has passed, transplant seedlings in rows 3½ to 4 feet apart, and about 12 inches apart in the row.

CULTURE: While plants are struggling to become established, remove weeds by hand as they appear. Once the vines begin to sprawl, the dense foliage will make further weeding unnecessary.

HARVEST: When the vines have been nipped by the first frost, carefully dig out roots with a spading fork. Allow tubers to dry several hours in the field, and then cure by placing them in containers and storing in a warm, well-ventilated room.

T

TOMATO

If there were such a thing as an all-star garden, there's no question that tomatoes would be the top vote-getter. Adaptable to any soil and promising almost guaranteed success, tomatoes will provide armfuls of delicious, vine-ripened fruit.

VARIETIES: Seed catalogues overflow with irresistible

photographs of the many varieties available. Some are early-bearers, others produce large, thin-skinned fruit, while still others are yellow and low in acid content. There are cherry or patio tomatoes, paste tomatoes, tomatoes grown for canning, and tomatoes developed for cooler regions. The best-known standard varieties include Beefsteak, Heinz, Rutgers, and New Yorker. Among the recommended hybrids are Moreton, Supersonic, Jet Star, Burpee's Big Boy, Big Girl, Early Girl, and Fireball. For cherry or cocktail tomatoes, try Small Fry, Pixie, Presto, or Sweet 100.

PLANTING: Tender and requiring a fairly long growing season, tomatoes usually are started indoors while winter is still in full swing. Eight to ten weeks before the frost-free date for your region, plant seed in flats, peat pots, or peat pellets filled with a sterile growing medium. Water thoroughly and cover with glass or plastic to conserve moisture.

If temperatures are right (between 70 and 80 degrees), the seeds will sprout within 10 to 14 days. Remove cover and put flats in a sunny window or under fluorescent lights. Be sure to turn window flats occasionally to keep plants growing straight. Two weeks before transplanting, harden-off plants by putting them in a cold frame. If a cold frame is not available, plants may be acclimated to outdoor conditions by leaving them on a porch or patio during the day. Since evening temperatures can get low enough to do harm, plants should be brought back indoors at night.

Any soil that has been adequately conditioned will support tomatoes. If manure or chemical supplements are used, it's best to stick with tomato food or vegetable-garden fertilizer. Follow package directions. Set plants that will be allowed to ramble about 2 feet apart in rows 3 feet apart. Staked or cage-supported tomatoes take up less space and can be placed closer together. Smaller varieties can be spaced every 12 to 15 inches in rows 15 inches apart. A 2-inch collar of cardboard or aluminum foil wrapped around the lower stem of each plant will discourage cutworm attacks. Shade plants with newspaper or cardboard immediately after planting if the sun seems especially glaring and hot. Water thoroughly.

CULTURE: Once plants become established, they will practically explode out of the ground, sending vines in all directions. To control foliage growth and encourage fruiting, it's best periodically to pinch off the suckers that sprout from the axils of the plant (the crotch where the leaf stem joins the main stem). At the same time, the plant will need some kind of support. Generally, stakes are inserted next to the plant, but wire cylinders, folding trellises, and portable racks are other ways support can be provided.

As weeds appear, remove them by hand near plants, and cultivate between rows. After stems have thickened, use a mulch to hold in soil moisture and smother emerging weeds. In cooler regions, a black plastic mulch will do everything other mulches do, and will keep soil temperatures on the warm side at the same time.

HARVEST: As soon as a pink blush is noticeable, it's only a matter of days before the fruit is ready for picking. A fully ripened tomato will practically drop into your hand. If any tugging or excessive pulling is necessary, the fruit is probably not completely ripe. As the season approaches its end, pinch off vine tips and any flower clusters to hasten ripening of green fruit. When frost threatens, green tomatoes may be taken inside, wrapped in newspapers, and stored in a cool place until they ripen. Destroy spent tomato vines to prevent diseases and pests from overwintering.

TURNIP
See rutabaga and turnip

W

WATERMELON

If space is at a premium, any plans for growing watermelon probably will have to be shelved until the garden expands. The long, ranging vines are prodigious space-consumers. In addition, the large fruit requires a long growing season in order to develop and mature. But for some gardeners, summer could never be complete without chilled slices of mouth-watering ruby-red watermelon.

VARIETIES: Seedsmen have constantly strived to develop improved strains of watermelon that will mature in less time and take up less room. Some types are seedless, while others have different colored flesh. Sugar Baby, for example, bears small, round fruits in about 86 days. Burpee's Sugar Bush grows on compact vines that bear mature fruit in about 80 days. New Hampshire Midget requires only 70 days from planting to harvest. Other popular varieties include Burpee's Fordhook, Crimson Sweet, Dixie Queen, Yellow Baby, and Charleston Gray.

PLANTING: As you might guess from the size of the plant and its fruit, watermelon is a heavy feeder, which means soil should be packed full of nutrient-rich materials such as compost or rotted manure. One way to get plants off to a good start is to place a shovelful or two of manure or compost under each hill, then mix a half a pound of commercial fertilizer into the soil you gather up. Plant four to five seeds per hill, 2 inches deep. Depending on the variety, hills should be spaced 6 to 8 feet apart.

CULTURE: A full-sized watermelon is practically all water (about 93 percent). As a result, soil moisture is a critical element. Water whenever rainfall falls below required levels. A black plastic mulch will help hold in moisture and at the same time keep soil temperatures on the high side. Once plants begin to vine, weeds will become less of a problem.

HARVEST: Experience is the best teacher when it comes to determining when a watermelon is at peak ripeness. Some say the fruits are ready when the undersides have turned a creamy yellow color. Others say the only reliable way to tell is by rapping the rind with the knuckles. A dull, hollow sound means the melon is ready for picking and eating.

OTHER MELONS: If you are lucky enough to have a long growing season, you might want to try one of the more unusual members of the melon family. Some of the best known include: honeydew, Persian, casaba, and crenshaw. All have the same cultural and harvesting requirements as watermelon.

The honeydew melon is prized for its pale green, juicy sweet meat. A slightly waxy, fragile, creamy-yellow rind and a pleasant aroma are guides to ripeness. Fruit weighs 4 to 6 pounds, and matures in about 110 days.

Persian melons are like giant cantaloupes. They weigh 4 to 8 pounds, have fine gray netting on their green rind, and produce vivid orange meat. They're mildly sweet—the rounder the melon, the sweeter the flavor. A smooth stem end and a distinctively pleasant aroma signal ripeness. Persian melons mature in about 95 days.

Casaba melons weigh 4 to 7 pounds, and have a globular shape that's sometimes pointed toward the stem. The flavor is subtle—mild and only slightly sweet. Ripe casabas have a deeply furrowed butter-yellow rind, soft creamy-white meat, and little aroma. This melon is a good keeper. Plants mature in about 120 days.

The crenshaw melon is a relative newcomer. It's a cross between the Persian and the casaba. The crenshaw averages about 4 to 8 pounds, and matures in about 95 days. It has green blotches when ripe.

Tomato Support Systems

One of the best ways to get early blemish-free tomatoes is to stake or support the vines. Tomato vines can be allowed to sprawl over a mulched area in the garden, but this will often result in later bearing and damaged fruit. Rambling tomato vines also take up a lot of valuable garden space.

One of the most popular ways to support a tomato vine is to contain the plant within a wire cage. Off the ground, the tomatoes won't rot and the plants' leaves provide enough shade to cut down on sunscald and fruit cracking. The fruit is also much easier to harvest.

One way to install a tomato cage is to dig a 2-foot-deep hole that's the diameter of the cage. Fill the hole with well-rotted compost, then set the cage around the perimeter, staking it firmly into the ground. Now, plant four tomatoes around the outside of the cage, tying them to the wire as they grow. The tomato roots will seek out the adjacent compost and feed well. And this arrangement also will conserve valuable garden space.

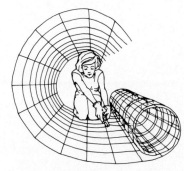

To make a tomato cage, you'll need to cut a 5-foot-wide section from a roll of concrete reinforcing wire. Try to find reinforcing wire that's at least 5 feet tall. Most tomato vines will quickly fill a cage of this size. If the plants get too tall, cages can be stacked.

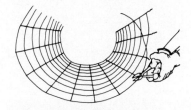

Remove the bottom rung of the wire so you can easily push the completed cage into the ground up to the second rung. This helps support the cage in high winds. And always be sure to wear sturdy gloves when working with reinforcing wire.

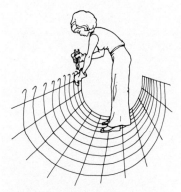

Use heavy-duty pliers to bend hooks along one side, as shown. Now simply hook up the sides to form the cage.

Place the cage over young tomato plants after they are established in the garden. It's a good idea to mulch all tomato plants before surrounding them with the wire cage. Be sure to push the cage firmly into the ground, and plant wooden stakes close to the base of the cage for added support. Tie the tomato cage to these stakes with wire or heavy twine to prevent toppling.

If you don't want to use wire cages, you also can stake tomato vines with sturdy wooden or metal poles. Drive the stakes into the ground before setting out young tomato plants; if you push them into the ground after plants are already growing, you're liable to damage tender root systems.

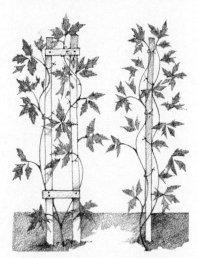

Single or cross-supported stakes can be used, but single stakes require more work to keep vines growing. Loosely attach tomato vines to the supports with figure-eight loops of old nylons or strips of cloth. Since side shoots can become unmanageable and delay fruiting, prune all staked plants so that only main stems develop.

Tomato How-To

Sun not only provides warmth and light, but also plays an important part in ripening. Tomatoes locked in deep shade turn red much slower than fruit exposed to sufficient sunlight. Stud es also have shown that tomatoes ripened in the sun have a higher vitamin C content.

The tomato is a vine plant, which means that stems and leaves will grow in all directions if left untrained. A popular method of checking plant growth while increasing the amount of sunlight striking fruit is "suckering"—that is, removing tiny stems that sprout from axils where leaf stems join the main stem.

As soon as plants become established in the garden, you'll notice a sudden spurt of new growth. This is the time to keep a sharp lookout for emerging suckers.

As soon as they are detected, grip them between the thumb and index finger and bend back and forth until they're detached. Take care not to cause undue injury to the remaining plant. And try to avoid pruning when plants are wet to prevent the spread of disease.

Pruning also can speed the ripening process when the season nears a close. Although suckers have been removed, you can help channel still more growing energy

into the fruit already on the vine by pinching off bloom clusters and tips of plants. Because frost is just around the corner, these blossoms will not have enough time to reach fruition.

When transplanting young seedlings, keep these points in

mind. Young plants cannot be rudely thrust into the soil to fend for themselves. Be sure to harden-off plants by holding them in a cold frame or by placing them on a porch or terrace during the day for at least ten days before transplanting.

It's important, too, to protect the roots as much as possible from the trauma of transplanting. Begin by watering thoroughly. Then cover plants with damp newspaper and shield from the direct rays of the sun while working in the garden. Plant only a few at a time so roots won't dry out while waiting for watering.

Cutworms are an always-possible menace. A collar constructed of stiff paper, aluminum foil, or tar paper should be placed around the stem of each plant and inserted at least ½ inch into the soil.

Because a tomato plant can send out roots from any part of its stem, there's little danger of planting seedlings too deep. In fact, tomatoes will get off to a better start if soil covers most of the lower stem. If the plants are extra "leggy," bury the entire stem lengthwise under the surface of the soil. Seedlings planted in this manner will quickly sprout along the entire length of the stem. Once soil has been pressed snugly around roots, ridge some soil around bases to collect water and give plants a generous watering.

49

Vegetable Know-How

It's usually the stems, leaves, blossoms, and fruit that preoccupy the gardener—not the soil. Soil, for many, is the stuff that sticks to your shoes or blows around as dust in the searing heat of midsummer. Yet in a sense, soil is the bottom line of all home gardening.

The first step for the vegetable grower is to get the soil in the proper condition to receive seeds and plants. But wait until the soil has had a chance to drain before spading or rototilling. As a test, simply squeeze a handful into a compact mass. If the soil crumbles easily when you let go, it's ready for working.

After the soil has been turned over, break up remaining clods and remove pieces of sod. Sticks, stones, roots, and other debris also should be carted away. Then rake the garden area to prepare the final seed bed.

Almost every soil can use a little help when it comes to improving fertility. Manures and other organic materials supply some nutrients, but are more useful as conditioners (see Composting, page 56). A commercial chemical fertilizer contains abundant amounts of the principal nutrients (nitrogen, potassium, and phosphorus) and is quick and inexpensive to use. Just before planting, apply fertilizer at the rate of about 4 to 5 pounds per 100 square feet of garden area. Then rake thoroughly into the upper 6 inches of soil.

When shopping for fertilizer, remember that different strengths are expressed by means of a numerical code. For example, a bag or container may simply be labeled 5-10-10. The first figure indicates the percentage of nitrogen; the second, phosphorus; and the third, potassium.

Your soil's pH—an index of acidity or alkalinity—is also important to those plants that have specific preferences. If your soil is on the acid side—and most soils are naturally acid—apply ground agricultural limestone at the rate of 5 to 6 pounds per 100 square feet.

If you're uncertain of the condition of your soil, contact your county extension office to arrange for a test at your nearest soil testing station. They'll give you a complete analysis.

Turn over your soil in the spring, or better yet, in the fall before it freezes.

A rotary tiller saves time and energy.

Rake seed bed smooth before planting.

SOIL AMENDMENT CHART

Material	Amount Per 100 Sq. Ft.	When to Apply	Benefits	Remarks
ORGANIC AMENDMENTS				
Cow, sheep, horse, or hog manure	3 to 5 bushels	Two weeks before planting	Good source of nitrogen; conditions soil	Allow to compost before using
Poultry (chicken, goose, duck, or turkey) manure	1 to 2 bushels	Two weeks before planting	Very high in nitrogen	Avoid over-application since excess amounts can "burn" roots
Compost	2 to 4 bushels	Two weeks before planting and as side-dressing	Provides major and minor nutrients; excellent soil conditioner	Screen thoroughly to remove clumps and other unrotted material
Peat moss	20 cubic feet	When preparing soil in spring	Contains no nutrients but is excellent soil conditioner	Work thoroughly into upper 6 inches of soil
FERTILIZERS				
Blood meal	10 ounces	One week before planting and as side-dressing	High in nitrogen (15%)	Also useful for discouraging small animal pests such as rabbits
Fish scraps	1¼ pounds	One week before planting and as side-dressing	High in all major nutrients: nitrogen (8%), phosphorus (13%), potassium (4%)	
Cottonseed meal	5 pounds	One week before planting and as side-dressing	High in nitrogen (8%) and phosphorus (2.5%)	Best for acid-loving plants
Bone meal	2½ pounds	Before or at planting time	High in phosphorus (24%); moderate in nitrogen (4%)	Steamed bone meal recommended; bone meal also helps reduce soil acidity
Wood ashes	4 pounds	Before or at planting time	High in potash (8%), with moderate amount of phosphorus	If allowed to stand, rain will leach out nutrients; work into soil immediately
GREEN MANURES				
Winter rye or vetch	Broadcast ¼ pound of seed over harrowed or raked soil	In fall after harvest and after all debris has been removed (early spring in southern regions)	Protects topsoil from erosion; provides nutrients when plowed under in spring; helps soil structure	Allow to grow to a height of 4 to 6 inches before turning under
Lime	5 pounds or as indicated by pH soil reaction test	Before soil is turned in spring; greater amounts should be divided into two applications	Indirectly improves soil structure; increases availability of soil nutrients	Avoid over-application
CHEMICAL AMENDMENTS				
Balanced fertilizer (5-10-10 or 5-10-5)	With manure, 3 to 4 pounds; without manure, 4 to 5 pounds	Rake thoroughly into top 4 inches of soil at planting or use as side-dressing	Provides nitrogen, phosphorus, and potassium for immediate use by plants	Contains few, if any, of the micronutrients; keep from direct contact with plant
Nitrate of soda	2 pounds per 100 feet of row	As side-dressing when plants are 4 inches high and every 2 weeks thereafter	Offers immediately available dose of nitrogen; especially recommended for leaf crops	Keep granules from coming into contact with leaves and roots
Ammonium sulfate	2 pounds per 100 feet of row	As side-dressing	Quick source of nitrogen; good for acid-loving plants	
Ammonium nitrate	1 pound per 100 feet of row	As side-dressing		

Getting Started

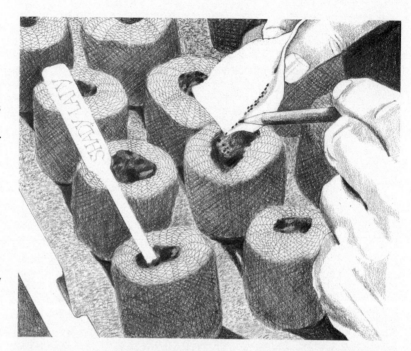

You'll be off to an earlier start this spring if you use one of the new plant-starter kits now on the market. These kits come complete with everything you'll need to produce stocky seedlings in a minimum of space. And as your seedlings grow, you can take your time planning their permanent garden locations. Just follow the simple instructions and you'll be setting out vegetables and enjoying flowers ahead of your procrastinating neighbors.

This seed-starting kit is practically a one-step affair—quick, clean, and efficient. The planters are net-enclosed peat moss balls that start out as flat disks. Soak them in

water for a few minutes until they swell to usable size. Then set them on a bed of milled peat and vermiculite, which is kept moist by a wick in the plastic reservoir. The water level to maintain is clearly visible, and pots kept moist in this way need only occasional gentle overhead watering.

Plant just two or three seeds in each pot by pressing seed lightly into the moist peat moss. When the seedlings show their first true leaves, thin out plants, leaving only the strongest one in each pot to mature. There's no need to fertilize, because the growing medium provides adequate plant food to last until the plants are set out in permanent garden locations.

Place the flat in a sunny window or under artificial lights in a growing unit, as shown here. If you use a

window spot, you'll need to turn the flat occasionally to avoid developing spindly plants. (You'll know when to turn the flat—the plants will lean toward the light.) With overhead artificial lights, you get sturdy plants that take off outdoors without any harmful setback.

Seedlings started in peat pots have the edge over those started in other containers. Transplanting shock is less, as the whole peat ball goes into the ground and roots are not disturbed. We combined petunias, impatiens, and ageratum with the excellent results you see here. Melons, tomatoes, and peppers also will benefit from an early start. Check our Vegetable ABCs section for starting times.

COLD FRAMES

Want a part-time greenhouse to extend your gardening season? It's as easy as building a box. The same basic structure can serve as either a cold frame or a hotbed. The cold frame is a bottomless box; the hotbed is much the same, but with the addition of a soil heating cable. Both types of frames utilize the sun's heat to warm the enclosed soil; the hotbed just adds finer control over soil temperature.

The south side of the house or garage is a good spot for your box. Or, put it in the shelter of a thick, high hedge or a board fence. But make sure the site you choose has a southern exposure to trap maximum sun and to shelter your

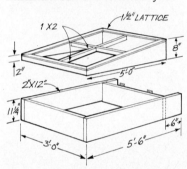

plants from predominantly northern spring winds. Good drainage is essential, too, so a level site is best. You can use sand or a soil mixture for the top layer within the frame. If you plan to do most of your planting in flats or pots, sand is fine. Some cuttings also will root in sand. But if you want to plant directly in the frame instead of in flats or pots, it's a good idea to make the top layer a soil mixture. A mixture of one part garden soil, one part sand, and one part peat or leaf mold is perfect.

For the base of either a cold frame or hotbed, build a 36x66-inch box, letting sides project 6 inches. Use 2x12 lumber, preferably redwood, cedar, or some other rot-resistant variety. If you choose nonresistant wood, treat it with a preservative other than creosote, which is hard on plants. The top of frame measures 36x60 inches, and the sides should taper from 2 to 8 inches.

Inside the top, center and fasten a piece of 1x2 lumber from side to

side; it should be flush with the top edge. Center and fasten another piece from front to rear, also flush with top edge, and lap-join where the 1x2s cross. This crossed structure will offer support for clear plastic sheeting.

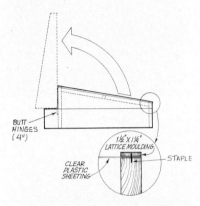

Hinge top to base with 4-inch butt hinges. When the top is fully open, it will rest on the 6-inch projections of the base sides. Use clear plastic or vinyl sheeting (6 to 8 mils thick) for the lid. Stretch and staple plastic to the lid edge, and then finish with lattice molding.

For a sun filter, build a frame of

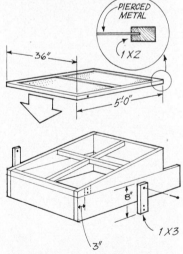

1x2 lumber and slot it to accept a piece of pierced sheet metal.

Attach two 8-inch pieces of 1x3 to the sides of the lid. The filter rests on the edge of the lid and is screwed to the 1x3s. This allows air passage between the filter and lid, and also allows the lid to be propped open to permit ventilation of the frame.

You'll also need covers for times

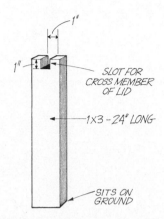

when frosts or freezes are expected. A number of products are available that will insulate against cold air. They come in rigid sheets, usually measuring 4x8 feet. These insulating materials are similar to composition board that is impregnated with a tar-like substance.

To make a cover, cut the material to fit the lid of the frame. Then lay

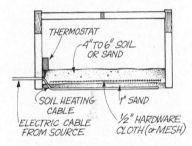

the cover on the lid and hold it down with several bricks or stones.

Cut a piece of 1x3 24 inches long to serve as a prop for the lid.

To turn a cold frame into a hotbed, add a soil-heating cable below the layer of sand or soil. Install the cable according to the manufacturer's directions.

To make your life easier, select a cable with a built-in thermostat so you don't have to tend the hotbed as often. In two or three months, this very small space can grow 20 or more trays of seedling varieties that otherwise might not be available at garden supply centers. For best results, try to locate your cold frame or hotbed along a south wall where it is protected from winds. There it can enjoy the warmth of the sun through most of the year.

Planting

There is an incredible life force locked inside a seed. When conditions are right, the seed bursts, sending forth an embryo root and stem. Each time, the same thing happens with mind-boggling

regularity. But the key to the process is giving the right seed the right conditions. Our task as gardeners is to bring seeds and these proper conditions together.

The most important elements needed for good germination are warmth and moisture. Ideally, the temperature should hover between 70 and 80 degrees Fahrenheit. Moisture is necessary to soften the hard seed shell and provide nutrients for the developing roots. But none of this can take place without soil.

Once the soil has been turned and fortified with lime, fertilizer, and organic matter (see Planning Basics, page 6), mark the exact location of the row. Place small stakes at each end, and stretch twine between them. Then, using the twine as a guide, dig a furrow with the corner of a hoe blade (or the handle end if a shallow furrow is needed). The idea is to plant seed at just the right depth. The deeper you go, the cooler the soil temperature; but the shallower the furrow, the drier the soil. A good rule of thumb is to plant seed at a depth equal to four times its diameter.

If seeds are small, take a pinch between thumb and index finger and sow by rubbing fingers together

over the furrow. Larger seeds can be planted individually. Cover seed with soil and tamp gently with your hand or the back of a hoe blade. Then remove twine and mark the row with an empty seed packet or plant labels. Water gently but thoroughly; if a dry spell occurs, soil moisture can be held constant by placing a thin mulch of dried lawn clippings or partially rotted compost over the row.

Once tiny sprouts have broken through the soil, care should be

taken to keep weeds from suffocating plants. Longer-germinating seeds can be mixed with a handful of radish seed so the quick-growing radish will help you locate the row. Then remove weeds in the row by hand. Spaces between rows can be cultivated lightly with a hoe, but keep cultivation shallow so tender roots aren't damaged.

When setting out young seedlings, mark rows with twine and dig holes at recommended intervals. Fill holes with water, allow them to drain, and set in plants after placing foil or paper collars around stems to prevent cutworm damage. Then fill in soil, being sure to eliminate unwanted air spaces, and tamp gently. If plants appear to be suffering from the intense sun, shade can be supplied by placing shields made of brush or small boards next to each plant. Water frequently.

Several steps can be taken to ensure that transplants get off to a good start. When handling seedlings, keep roots from wind and sun so they won't dry out. If possible, transplant on a cloudy day.

Watering

Now it's possible to weather a severe drought and maintain a thriving garden at the same time. Trickle or drip irrigation is the secret. It's a system designed to make a little water go a long way.

The basic principle is simple. Water is delivered in small quantities under low pressure directly to where it does the most good—the root zones of the plants.

This water trickles through the soil by capillary action. Most air pas-

sages in the soil remain open, in contrast to the flooding of furrow irrigation or over-sprinkling. Thus, oxygen is always available to the roots, and the stresses of over-watering are eliminated.

Trickle irrigation is one of the best ways to conserve water. Little is lost to evaporation or runoff, especially if the unit is buried under a layer of mulch. If you don't have a ready source of organic matter for use as a mulch, rolled black plastic will do. The black plastic is especially effective spread under heat-loving crops such as melons, tomatoes, and peppers.

Trickle irrigation systems vary from dealer to dealer; the one shown above consists of ½-inch polyethylene header pipe and a roll of thin tape-like porous tubing.

The header pipe connects to a garden hose and routes water through the garden. It may be placed down the center of the garden, or along one end. The header pipe is then punctured with

a screwdriver at intervals corresponding to each garden row. Small 8- to 10-inch pieces of rubber connecting hose are inserted into these holes, with the other end of the connecting hose attached to a length of porous tape.

Roll out the tape along each vegetable bed, cutting it the same length as the row. Then crimp the end of the tape to prevent water loss when the system is in use.

Porous irrigation tape is best placed about 3 to 4 inches away from the base of the plants. It's often a good idea to plant a double row of vegetables, placing the tape down the center.

To water, simply turn on the garden hose for several hours a day, letting water slowly ooze from the

porous tape. Pump only clean water; dirty water will clog the tape. And always keep the soil slightly moist; overly wet soil can be as detrimental as dry soil to healthy plant growth.

Most trickle irrigation systems come equipped with a ball valve or pressure emitter to regulate water

pressure within the system. Too much water pressure will result in blowouts and split tapes, while low pressure causes inefficient operation. It's a good idea to keep the system's water pressure somewhere between 3 and 4 pounds per square inch.

In the fall, clean the porous tape and connecting tubes and store in a dry place. The header pipes may be left intact over the winter.

Weather Breakers

We can juggle seeds around, move the garden from one spot to another, and even make a semblance of rain with the garden hose. But there's nothing we can do about the weather. If the sun shines, all is well. But if a cold snap moves in earlier than expected and turns the garden into a sea of wilted leaves, we have little recourse except to hope for better luck next year.

However, something can be done to lessen the effects of adverse weather. For instance, you can reduce the harmful effects of wind and temperature simply by choosing a good location for your vegetable garden. And by making

plant protectors from discarded cans and other containers, you can bring your best tomato plants through the first killing frost. You can even assemble pieces of scrap lumber to build portable, plastic-covered greenhouses that can be simply and easily placed over an entire row of seedlings.

Choosing a Site. Before setting spade to soil, take a close look at your property and assess the lay of the land. With proper placement of the garden, you can make considerable headway against the vicissitudes of the weather. For example, cool air tends to flow toward lower elevations, while warm air rises. Try to locate your garden on high ground so tender plants won't suffer from cold air settling in pockets of ground. Also take stock of the trees on your property and the direction of the prevailing winds. Try to snuggle your garden up to a tree line where winds won't be as strong, or take advantage of a garage or shed as a windbreak.

Keep in mind that a slope facing south receives more direct sun and is much warmer than a northern slope. In the spring, snow will melt sooner and soil will warm quicker on southern exposures. So if possible, try to place rows so they run from north to south in order to expose plants to equal sunshine.

Fending Off Frost. The most important calendar dates to the vegetable grower are the average last day of frost in the spring and the average first day of frost in the fall—the two dates that determine the length of the growing season.

There are several ways to determine these times for your particular area. You can consult neighbors who have been gardening for a long time, or simply trust your luck to trial and error. However, your best bet is to consult the nearest agricultural county extension office or to send for frost date material from the U.S. Government Printing Office.

There's nothing magical about frost-free dates. The United States Weather Bureau has been tabulating and recording frost dates all over the country since 1899. With that much information, it's possible to make fairly accurate estimates of when and where frost will strike for the last time in the spring and for the first time in the fall.

But the terrain surrounding your area also can have an effect. For example, if you're near a large body of water, temperatures will not change as rapidly as elsewhere since water temperatures remain much more constant. If you live in a slight depression, you might find cool air slipping down from higher ground and settling on your garden, bringing freezing temperatures with it. Keep these factors in mind when obtaining advice.

There are many ways to prevent freezing temperatures from

penetrating the leaves of plants and killing their cells. Cover small seedlings with inverted coffee cans or plastic half-gallon milk bottles that have had their bottoms cut out. Lift the can daily for light. Bushel baskets, cardboard boxes, and even newspaper tents held down with soil or small stones can be effective at keeping frost out and warmth in. Many gardeners who are loyal to the benefits of mulch keep enough between their rows so that a layer can be pulled gently over plants whenever frost threatens.

Remember, though, that plants will literally bake inside protectors in

tender seedlings to the garden. Young plants, pampered by indoor or greenhouse conditions, may have spent only a week or two in a cold frame to harden-off. Small wonder that they wilt at the shock of being thrust into the unpredictable elements. As soon as plants are in the ground, water thoroughly and insert protectors as defense against high winds and burning sun. But proper ventilation also is essential, so prop open your protectors right after sunrise and keep them open all day long.

Sun, sun, and more sun is relished by most vegetables, especially fruiting crops such as tomatoes. But the handful of vegetables that are grown for greens, such as spinach, lettuce, chard, and mustard, only bolt to seed in warm weather. And cool temperatures generally mean slower growth.

One way to blunt the piercing sun is to construct lattice coverings. Simply nail strips of lath material on

Portable Greenhouses. The dread of every gardener is unexpected frost. Days of planning, hard work, and money can go up in mist as a result of a few hours of freezing temperatures. Frost also defines the length of the season. But you can foil frost by constructing lightweight, portable greenhouses that can be set in place over tender plants in a matter of minutes. Greenhouses also let you extend your growing season by as much as a month to a month and a half.

Build a light frame of 2x2s or reinforced 1x3s connected with pins or hinges. Next, staple clear plastic to frame edges, and if desired, attach separate pieces of plastic to the ends to form a complete enclosure. Use heavy gauge plastic to prevent tearing by heavy winds. Then, in the spring when patches of snow still linger in the shadows, you can start planting under warm greenhouse conditions.

In the late summer, replant the greenhouse area with cool-season crops like lettuce, spinach, radishes, Swiss chard, and beets for a harvest that will last well into the fall and winter months.

Where winters are severe, the unit can be easily removed from the garden, folded, and stored for another season of use. In warmer climates, it can be used all year.

the warmth of the morning sun. Remove your coverings as soon as possible the next day. And if by chance frost sneaks up on you and you discover a white covering on your prized plants, water sprinkled from the garden hose can sometimes save your crops.

Weather breakers also are useful when it comes time to transplant

a 2x2 frame at 2-inch intervals. Your shade frame should be a minimum of 18 inches wide and 12 inches high. The partial shade it creates will also help keep soil temperature down. For other shade solutions, bend a section of snow fencing over entire rows, or push a wood shingle into the soil on the south side of each plant.

Mulching

If it weren't for weeds, gardening would be a joy forever. Trouble is, the soil is packed with tiny weed seeds waiting to break into growth. And as soon as an emerging crop is nipped with a hoe, a new batch appears from the seeds that have been stirred up.

But the battle isn't hopeless. Mulch—material placed around plants—also is one of the most effective devices for weed control. By depriving unwanted weeds of essential sunlght, mulch causes weed seedlings to languish and die. Those that do manage to push through are weak and spindly and are easy to pull by hand. Mulch has numerous invisible benefits as well:

• Mulch preserves soil moisture. By shielding the topsoil from the direct rays of the sun, it drastically slows the rate of water evaporation.

• A loose, well-maintained mulch acts as insulation, keeping soil temperatures on the cool side. Cool-season crops like cabbage, broccoli, cauliflower, and Brussels sprouts can be helped through midsummer heat if snuggled in mulch.

• In some respects, spreading mulch over the soil is like starting a compost pile right in the garden. The organic material nearest the soil will gradually break down and add valuable humus to the garden.

• The moist darkness under a mulch is a near-perfect haven for earthworms. Tunneling and foraging worms aerate the soil and create pore spaces where water can penetrate.

• Mulch also keeps fruits and vegetables from becoming mud-splattered during heavy rains.

Black plastic mulch is ideal for warmth-loving melons. Cut holes for plants and for drainage of rainfall.

In addition, a mulch cushion reduces soil compaction.

But, as with almost everything, mulch has its drawbacks. If not properly applied, mulch can turn into a dense layer that restricts the free passage of water. It can keep temperatures too low, bringing warmer season crops to a standstill. Also, by bringing together excessive moisture and rotting material, it can invite the spread of certain fungus diseases. And, some mulching material may cause nitrogen deficiency, necessitating supplemental applications of commercial fertilizer.

But almost anything can be used as a mulch, providing it's porous and easy to manage (see the mulching chart, opposite). Begin your mulching program as soon as possible by putting aside the material early in the season. After plants are about 4 inches high, carefully lay mulch around bases and between rows. For warm-season vegetables, wait until the soil has thoroughly warmed. Then, as the season progresses, add fresh material so mulch remains about 3 inches thick.

Or, lay black plastic before sowing seed or setting out transplants. Cut holes where seeds or seedlings are to be planted, and sprinkle with a garden hose. After a rain, make punctures in areas of standing water.

If plants begin to look sickly and a trifle yellow around the edges, it may mean the breakdown of organic mulch is robbing the soil of available nitrogen. Simply sprinkle a high-nitrogen fertilizer as a side-dressing alongside each row.

A 6-inch layer of straw is placed in and around growing vegetables to preserve soil moisture and to keep weeds at a minimum. Decaying organic matter also adds needed plant food and keeps soil from baking. Although a wide variety of materials can be used for mulch, make sure the soil has warmed before applying them.

Mulch Chart

Material	Source	Recommended Depth	Characteristics
Cocoa bean shells	Candy manufacturers or garden supply centers	3 to 4 inches	Light in weight, pleasing in appearance, and of good fertilizing value. Initial chocolate odor fades after two weeks. May be mixed with sawdust (2 parts shells to 1 part sawdust) to prevent caking.
Corncobs (ground)	Corn-growing areas	4 to 6 inches	Coarse material with good moisture retention qualities. Can harbor injurious insect pests. Somewhat slow to break down.
Grass clippings	Lawn	2 to 3 inches	Allow to stand 2 or 3 days before using to avoid burning plants with decomposition heat. May be mixed with coarse material to reduce matting.
Hay	Farmers, cut fields, garden supply centers	6 to 8 inches	Leguminous grasses (alfalfa, clover) decay faster and supply nitrogen. Salt hay is useful because seeds will not sprout in garden soil.
Leaves	Deciduous trees	6 to 8 inches	Tends to become matted and soggy if not allowed to compost before applying. May be used immediately when mixed with another material, such as grass clippings. Oak leaves are best for acid-loving plants.
Manure (mixed with straw)	Dairy farms or stables	4 to 6 inches	Should be partially composted before applying to prevent burning plants. Good nutrient source.
Peanut shells	Peanut-growing areas, especially the South	2 to 4 inches	Easy to apply, but may have to be mixed with heavier material or weighted down with a layer of coarse mulch.
Peat moss	Garden supply centers	3 to 5 inches	Good soil conditioner, but lacking in nutrients. May dry out and repel water. Keep moist or mix with another material to avoid crusting.
Pine needles	Coniferous trees	2 inches	Excellent for strawberries and wildflowers. Will not be displaced by the wind. Decidedly acid. Allows free passage of rainfall and does not absorb moisture from the soil.
Plastic film (black)	Hardware stores and garden supply centers		Especially useful for large areas. Excellent for preserving moisture. Will warm soil (as opposed to organic materials that slow warming). Will last 4 or 5 years if properly anchored. Punch holes at low points to allow water penetration.
Sawdust	Sawmills and lumberyards	1 to 2 inches	Excellent general mulch and soil conditioner. Apply nitrogen fertilizer at regular intervals to prevent depletion of soil nitrogen.
Straw	Farms, feed stores, and garden supply centers	4 to 6 inches	Coarser than hay, and longer lasting. Practical for large areas, such as the corn or pumpkin patch.
Tobacco stems	Tobacco farms	6 to 8 inches	Fairly high in nitrogen and potassium. A coarse material. Can repel insects.
Wood chips	Local utility operation, home shredder, or street department	3 to 4 inches	Much coarser than sawdust, and less likely to cause nitrogen deficiency.

Staking and Supporting Crops

Supporting and staking plants may require a little extra effort at the outset, but once harvest begins, the rewards are quickly evident. You'll find fruits are cleaner because their elevation keeps them from getting splashed with mud during heavy rains. Disease will be almost nonexistent because air circulation is better and fruit doesn't rest on the soil where disease spores can easily spread. And, your produce may ripen sooner since the sun is not blocked by a thicket of leaves.

For the homeowner strapped for space, vertical gardening can mean bumper crops where vegetable growing was formerly considered impossible. Poles, trellises, fencing material, and even twine can be used to train vines to grow in any desired direction. Here are some staking and support ideas that you can easily adapt to your particular needs and the crops you plan to grow this season.

Bean Tepee. Yields can be quadrupled by encouraging beans to grow in the air. Pole varieties grow as high as 7 feet if given plenty of support and an abundance of soil nutrients. Simply construct a tepee shape using three 8-foot poles made from young saplings, 1x1-inch lath, or furring strips. Push them an inch or so into the ground and plant six to eight seeds at the base of each pole. When plants are about 4 inches high, thin to four or five healthy seedlings per pole.

Cucumber, Squash, and Melon Racks. A cement retaining wall or

Some crops send out snakelike vines that creep along the ground in all directions. The fruits are usually large and develop at regular intervals along the vine. Unfortunately for the home gardener with a shortage of space, these vine crops consume too much room to be practical. But vines aren't fussy; they're as happy growing up a wall or along a fence as they are sprawling across the ground over neighboring vegetables.

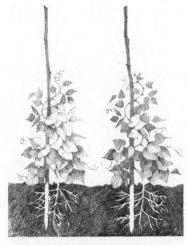

to be expensive. After rooting through a shed, attic, or garage, a good scavenger can usually come up with all that's needed. Look for old snow fence, iron posts, discarded pipe, or lath taken from an old house. Or visit the town dump where contractors dispose of useless building materials. And if they're available, use large-size prunings from trees and shrubs: your crops get needed support while your trees get a grooming.

unsightly fence can be turned into a vegetable paradise when utilized as a support for any of the melon crops, squash, or cucumber. Remember, though, that your plants should be placed on the south side so that sunlight is always plentiful.

Simply construct a wooden rack out of 2x3s and lath (see opposite page), and secure it to a wall or fence. As plants send out vines, carefully tie them to the wood strips. Once fruits begin to form, you'll have to check them frequently. Since ripening fruit can become so heavy that it drops off the vine, support it with slings made from discarded nylon stockings or netting suspended from the frame. Make a trellis to place over plants to keep ripening produce off the ground. And staple special nylon netting to 2x2 posts for vines, as shown at right. Staple the net to the first post, stretch it taut, and staple to the second post. Continue until the fence is complete. If you don't have a staple gun, use U-shaped nails.

Supporting material doesn't have

Composting

To the untrained eye, a compost heap appears to be nothing more than a tangled mess of garden garbage. But to the veteran gardener, compost is one of the most precious materials to be found within a shovel's throw of the garden. Not only does it help condition the soil, but it also contains many trace elements unavailable in any other form.

Basically, the composting process is nothing more than an accelerated version of what goes on in nature. Leaves, twigs, dead grass, and other organic materials are attacked by billions of microorganisms when they come into contact with the soil. With the proper amounts of heat, air, water, and nitrogen, nature's wastes are gradually reduced to a form that can be utilized by plants. In short, nothing really ever dies; it's simply recycled.

Locating the Compost Pile. A shady spot to one side of the garden is an ideal place for compost because finished material easily can be incorporated into the soil, and the shade will help keep the pile moist. Try to locate near a water supply so new garden refuse can be moistened as it's added. And, avoid piling material against your house, garage, or favorite fence; compost

useful in making a base for the heap, but should not be used unless they are shredded. Leaves also are excellent, but either should be mixed with hay or ground up to prevent matting. Sawdust, garden refuse, kitchen waste (except bones and greasy materials), and animal waste are all possible ingredients. Weeds,

too, are fine, since the pile usually develops sufficient heat to destroy mature seeds.

Making the Bin. You'll hasten the decay process and make the finished product much easier to reach if you construct a bin. All that's needed is three sides of wire mesh fastened to stakes set in the ground.

can harbor wood-rotting fungi.

What to Put in the Compost Bin. Almost anything that grows out of the ground can be used for compost. But remember—the smaller the particles, the quicker they will decompose. Cornstalks are

The fourth side should consist of planks that can be removed individually for ease in adding material and taking it out. Many gardeners prefer to make two bins, so compost can be easily aerated by forking it from one bin to the other.

Shown on this page are small piles contained in ornamental fencing; a permanent bin made from concrete blocks held in place by iron-pipe stakes at the corners; and large wire bins showing construction details for the slatted board fronts.

Constructing the Compost Pile. Once the location has been picked, dig a shallow trench about 4 feet square and fill with twigs, brush, or cornstalks. Then add a 10- to 12-inch layer of organic material, such as lawn clippings, leaves, or garden waste, and sprinkle with water. Cap with a layer of cow or horse manure topped by an inch or two of soil that was removed from the trench. Finally, add about a cupful of lime and a cupful of commercial 5-10-10 fertilizer. Be sure to water each layer of material thoroughly. Repeat until the pile is no more than 5 feet in height. In a matter of days, the pile will begin to heat up, which means the decay process is in full swing. Check occasionally to make sure the heap is moist, and after about two weeks, turn the pile over so contents are thoroughly aired.

Controlling Animal Visitors

If only a row or two of greens is planted, consider placing portable cages of welded wire mesh or chicken wire over each row. The cage pictured below is nothing more than wire fencing material bent to fit over crops. Or, a lightweight wood frame covered with plastic netting can be used instead.

Sometimes the entire garden comes under attack, which means that some kind of fencing may have to be erected. Simply hammer treated wood posts or steel poles into the ground at 4- to 6-foot intervals and attach wire fencing. If woodchucks are the chief villains, sink wire at least 6 inches into the ground to discourage burrowing. If netting or light wire is used, fence can be easily rolled up and stored at the end of the season.

When designing your fence, remember that vegetables need good air circulation to prevent the spread of diseases. The fencing material you choose should be open enough to provide proper ventilation. Weeds, too, should be kept down to foil insect pests and to eliminate breeding places for fungi.

If a vision of hordes of feasting animals threatens your peace of mind, remember that the pest you think is devouring your crops actually may be your best ally. Birds consume hundreds of insects a day, skunks spend their nights scooping grubs out of the ground, and snakes hunt down rodents (see Know Your Garden Allies, page 60). In fact, most gardeners will have more than enough surplus harvest to cover any incidental losses caused by animal or insect visitors. Perhaps we should simply grow a little more so everybody is satisfied.

Once plants break through the soil, you can be sure some watchful eyes besides your own are trained on the vegetable patch. Rabbits, squirrels, woodchucks, raccoons, and birds are quick to zero in on new delicacies appearing in the environment. In a single meal, a woodchuck can reduce your bean patch to a row of pathetic stubble.

Some gardeners, mindful of the ecology, plant a row of greens completely around the garden, hoping that nibblers won't go any further. Others circle the garden with dried blood, old shoes, and sometimes—in pure desperation—electrified wire.

Theories and tricks abound. But one of the best solutions is to put especially vulnerable vegetables like cabbage, lettuce, chard, and other greens inside a cage. The crop cage shown above, constructed in only a few hours, fits snugly over a raised bed of salad greens. Measuring 72x45 inches, the frame is made of 2x2s with triangles cut from ½-inch plywood as corner braces. After hinges were added to the top, wire mesh was stapled to the frame.

Know Your Garden Allies

Many creatures inhabit your garden—some harmful, others benign. But the fact is, you need both types in order to maintain the balance of nature. Only when vegetarian insects become numerous enough to damage your garden yield do they become pests. Without them, the beneficial creatures who depend upon them for food would vacate the area, leaving your garden susceptible to any new invasion of chewing, sucking insects.

Who are these garden allies? They include spiders, birds, and toads, as well as the many insects that gobble up or parasitize their vegetarian relatives in amazing numbers.

CANNIBAL INSECTS

Ladybug (8). Probably the best known of these garden benefactors is the ladybug—which is actually a beetle, not a bug, and is more properly called a lady beetle or ladybird. The most common variety sports 12 or 13 black spots on its reddish back. Both the adult ladybug and the larvae (juvenile stage) consume vast quantities of soft-bodied insects such as aphids, mealybugs, leafhoppers, scale insects, and the eggs and larvae of these and other small pests. A single ladybug will eat 50 aphids a day—and never tire of them as a steady diet.

Praying mantis (6). Not as colorful, but more dramatic in shape, and with an equally voracious appetite, is the stately praying mantis. Its name refers to the way the mantis stands, poised to grab an unsuspecting aphid, caterpillar, grasshopper, or whatever soft-bodied insect unsuspectingly wanders by.

Both ladybug and praying mantis egg cases can be ordered by mail from various nurseries around the country. A quart of hungry ladybugs should be enough for a large garden. A mantis egg case will contain upwards of 200 eggs; these will hatch when the weather is warm enough to bring out the native insects that make up the entire diet of the patient but extremely hungry mantis fledglings.

Lacewing (3). You'll know the lacewing by its seemingly oversize, pale green, gauzy wings and red-gold, beady eyes. It's also called aphid lion because of its fondness for those delectable green meals, but it won't turn up its nose at a chance to eat a mealybug, mite, or thrip.

Ground beetle (7). Ever turn over a board or stone and see a metallic or iridescent, dark-colored beetle dart away? Chances are it was a ground or carabid beetle, which thrives on slugs, caterpillars, and other destructive insects.

Syrphid fly (2). Adult syrphid flies are bright yellow and black, and may be mistaken for bees, as they also hover over flowers to feed on the nectar, thus helping with pollination.

The syrphid fly lays long white eggs among groups of aphids. The larvae that emerge are brown, gray, or mottled, and resemble slugs. One syrphid fly larva can destroy aphids at a rate of one per minute for long periods of time.

Firefly (5). Remember chasing these flashing fantasies on summer nights and bottling them up for psychedelic light shows? (Oxidation of a substance called luciferin in a heatless reaction produces the flashes of light that some authorities claim are mating signals.) Also called lightning bugs, fireflies are really beetles whose favorite feasts include cutworms, snails, and slugs.

Dragonfly (4) and damselfly. The exotic dragonfly and its delicate cousin, the damselfly, are both beautiful and beneficial. As they fly, their legs form basketlike nets to capture small insects, which are eaten on the wing as the predators continue their flights. Before "winning their wings," the young damselflies and dragonflies consume vast quantities of mosquitoes and other water insects. (Bless any living creature that helps keep down the mosquito population!)

Soldier beetles. Don't mistake a soldier beetle for a firefly—even though the two share a superficial resemblance. Soldier beetles have no light-producing organs. They feed primarily on aphids, mealybugs, and other small insects, but they will also eat plant tissues. You may find soldier beetles on large, showy flower

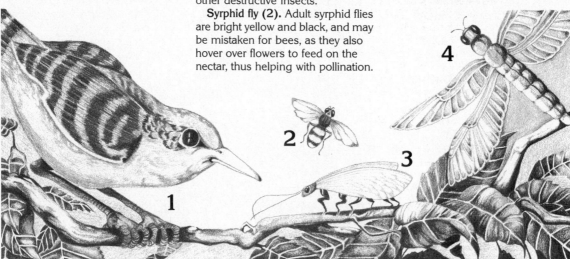

clusters such as goldenrod and elderberry, since the beetles will also feed on pollen and nectar.

Assassin bugs. Since they're not very specific in their hunting, assassin bugs sometimes kill beneficial insects such as honeybees. But they feed on a variety of caterpillars and leafhoppers, as well as Japanese beetles, so their overall effect should be considered positive. And though we hope you don't need them for such a purpose, one type of assassin bug will enter houses and feed on bloodthirsty bedbugs.

Robber flies. Grabbing a meal in flight is not at all uncommon for robber flies. They prey on flying insects—catching their prey with their legs—and sometimes attacking species almost as large as themselves. Flies, beetles, butterflies, moths, and spiders are among the delicacies in their diet.

Sphecid wasp. This is one of many groups of friendly wasps. The adults capture a wide variety of spiders, grasshoppers, caterpillars, aphids, bugs, and flies, and store them in small cells or compartments with their eggs. Thus, when the eggs hatch, the young wasps find a waiting supply of food.

PARASITE INSECTS

Trichogramma wasp. Among the parasitic insects, the trichogramma wasp is tiny but effective. The adult has a wingspread of only about 1/50th of an inch. Trichogramma lays its minute eggs inside the eggs of some 200 species of harmful pests, including tomato and cabbage worms and fruit moths. The larger host eggs are destroyed before the vegetarian larvae can emerge to eat leaves. Trichogramma wasp larvae are available by mail order.

Braconid wasp. This small parasite zeroes in on aphids and the larvae of many beetles and moths (including tent caterpillars and cutworms). The white egg-shaped cocoons you see attached to a tomato hornworm are often the pupae of wasps that went through the larval stage inside the worm's body—after the eggs were deposited there by an adult wasp.

Trachinid fly. These parasites resemble overgrown houseflies and are found resting on foliage or flowers. The eggs of trachinid flies are placed on the bodies of the insects they will parasitize or on the foliage where the insect will eat the eggs along with the leaf. The larvae feed internally on their hosts— which almost always die. They are especially useful for controlling gypsy and browntail moths, cutworms, armyworms, Japanese beetles, and European earwigs.

Chalcids. A family of minute or very small wasps, chalcids are parasites. But since they sometimes parasitize beneficial insects, they are a mixed blessing. They prey upon the larvae of beetles, moths, flies, and butterflies.

POLLINATORS

Among the allies in your garden, you'll find a variety of insects that are important for helping pollinate your plants.

Honeybees are, without doubt, the best-known and most dependable pollinators in your garden. It's been estimated that bees are responsible for more than 80 percent of all the pollination done by insects.

The honeybees, busy as they are, shouldn't get all of the credit, though. There are at least 5,000 species of bees in North America alone, and bumblebees, carpenter bees, alkali bees, and leafcutter bees are all effective pollinators.

Many of the other insects you'll find in your garden also help out with pollination. If you check, you'll find that butterflies, moths, wasps, gnats, and beetles are working *for* you.

OTHER GARDEN ALLIES

Spider (10). This shy arachnid is also a helpful ally in the garden, since its diet consists mainly of insects. The golden orb spider, for example, helps eradicate Japanese beetles from raspberry bushes. The brown wood spider that builds its nest in garden mulch has an insatiable appetite for grasshoppers.

Wren (1). Many birds like to augment their insect diets with your fruits, berries, and vegetables. But the friendly wren is first and foremost an insect-eater, with a proclivity for leafhoppers, plant lice, scale insects, whiteflies, and even the tiniest insect eggs. Install a wren house near your garden to encourage nesting.

Titmice and *bushtits* are other small birds whose favorite foods are similar to the wren's. *Purple martins* and *swallows* scoop up flies, wasps, and other bugs on the wing. A birdbath of regularly freshened water will attract birds to your garden.

Toad (9). Despite the fairy tales, don't kiss the picturesque toad if you're lucky enough to find one in your garden. If it turns into a handsome prince or princess, you've lost a real garden ally. During the night, toads eat just about any pest that moves, especially cutworms, slugs, and potato beetles. One toad devours up to 15,000 insects in one garden season. Provide a shallow container of water to encourage toads to remain in your garden.

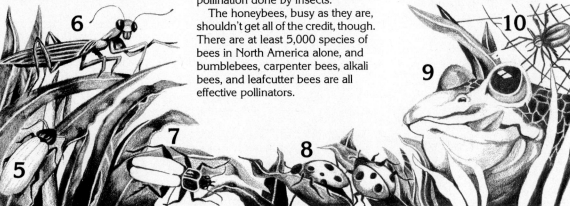

65

Pests and Problems

Not all is peaches and cream in the home garden. Often in a matter of a few agonizing days, insects and disease can threaten a season of dreams and hard work.

But just because a cluster of unknown bugs appears in your garden, you needn't toss hoe and rake aside in resignation. Insects, both bad and good, have exaggerated reputations. Most are kept in check by natural predators, as well as limited food supplies. But more importantly, insect pests usually gravitate toward unhealthy, defenseless plants. So the healthier and cleaner your garden, the less likely you are to come under insect attack. Here are some simple ways to keep vegetables in shape.

When thumbing through a seed catalog, pay special attention to those varieties that are advertised as "disease-resistant." Note, too, whether the seeds you order or buy at a garden center are treated for soil-borne diseases.

Keep weeds in check—and not only the ones that invade the garden, but also those that surround it.

Remove and destroy garden rubbish as soon as possible after harvest. But stay out of the vegetable patch when plants are wet.

If a menacing bug appears, check any impulse to blast it off with the strongest stuff around. First be sure you know what the insect is, and then use the safest spray that will do the job. In the chart below, you'll find a listing of common insects and the crops they attack, with recommended natural and chemical controls.

Disease and Pest Control Chart

Crop	Symptoms	Disease/Pest	Natural Control	Chemical Control
Asparagus	Pinched and distorted spears.	Cutworm	Plant tansy between asparagus rows.	Sevin. Spray before planting, when seedlings emerge, or when damage is evident.
	Light orange pustules on stems.	Rust	Plant a rust-resistant variety.	Maneb. Spray ferns after harvest.
Beans	Borings in seed and young plants.	Seed maggot	Use treated seed. Plant after soil becomes warm.	Diazinon. Apply to furrows or hills before planting.
	Leaves and seedpods damaged.	Mexican bean beetle	Hand-pick beetles from plants and destroy. Plant marigolds alongside or among bean rows.	Rotenone or Sevin or Malathion. Spray entire plant when beetles appear.
	Withered and discolored leaves.	Leafhopper		Sevin or Malathion. Spray plants, especially undersides of leaves, when insects appear.
Beets and Chard	White, threadlike tunnels within leaf layers.	Leaf miner		Malathion. Spray leaves thoroughly and repeat if necessary.
	Small, round spots on leaves.	Leaf spot	Use treated seed. Rotate crops after season of extensive injury.	Captan. Spray plants when damage occurs.
Cabbage Cauliflower Broccoli Brussels Sprouts	Ragged holes in leaves	Cabbageworm or Looper	Hand-pick loopers and drop into kerosene or hot water. Or use biological insecticide, *bacillus thuringiensis*.	
Cabbage	Curled leaves and discoloration.	Aphids	Remove with blast from garden hose or spray with water mixed with non-detergent soap.	Diazinon. Spray both sides of leaves when insects first appear.

Disease and Pest Control Chart

Crop	Symptoms	Disease/Pest	Natural Control	Chemical Control
Cabbage (con'd.)	General wilting of plants.	Cabbage maggot	Use treated seed and rotate crops.	Diazinon. Drench soil around plants after planting.
	Large, thick swellings on roots and stunted plants.	Clubroot	Avoid planting in infested soil. Rotate crops.	Terrachlor. Drench soil around roots of large seedlings when they are transplanted to garden.
Carrots, Parsnips, and Turnips	General wilting from damaged roots.	Rust fly		Diazinon. Drench furrow at planting time.
	Root and stem borings.	Carrot weevil	Rotate crops.	Diazinon. Spray seedlings when 2 to 3 inches high and at 10- to 14-day intervals.
	Brown or black spots on leaves.	Leaf blight	Rotate crops and avoid excess moisture.	Maneb. Spray six weeks after planting and repeat at 7- to 10-day intervals.
Corn	Damaged silks and ears.	Earworm	Place 2 or 3 drops of mineral oil into each ear when silks first begin to appear.	Sevin. Begin spraying when silks start to show; repeat four times at 2-day intervals.
	Collapsed tassels; single hole at tip or base of ear.	Borer	Check stalks and hand-pick worms each day. At end of season, gather and remove old stalks.	Sevin. Spray at 5- to 7-day intervals when tassels begin to form; repeat three times.
Cucumbers Muskmelon Pumpkin Squash Watermelon	Chewed leaves eventually skeletonized.	Striped cucumber beetle	Remove beetles by hand as they appear. Plant nasturtiums or radish among plants.	Rotenone or Sevin. Begin weekly sprayings as soon as plants emerge. Be sure to spray undersides of leaves.
	Damaged leaves, stalks. buds, flowers, and fruits.	Pickleworm and Melonworm		Sevin. When damage occurs, spray weekly.
	Crinkled and wilted vines.	Squash or Vine borer	Remove by hand wherever possible.	Rotenone or Sevin. Spray at weekly intervals as soon as seedlings have emerged.
	Wilted and curled leaves.	Squash bug	Destroy egg clusters; trap insects by placing board on soil near plants. Hand-pick mature beetles. Scatter nasturtiums among plants.	Sevin. Spray when insects appear and at weekly intervals.
Eggplant, Pepper, and Tomato	Small pinholes in leaves.	Flea beetle		Sevin. Spray plants thoroughly, including undersides of leaves, when beetles appear. Repeat two or three times.

Disease and Pest Control Chart (continued)

Crop	Symptoms	Disease/Pest	Natural Control	Chemical Control
Eggplant, Pepper, and Tomato (cont'd.)	Plants severed at soil line.	Cutworm	Wrap collar of aluminum foil or stiff paper around stem of each plant and insert 1 inch into soil.	Sevin. Dust or spray soil around plants in early evening.
	Chewed leaves and fruits	Tomato hornworm	Remove by hand and drop into container of kerosene.	Sevin. Spray plants thoroughly when worms appear.
	Curled and wilted leaves.	Aphids	Remove with blast from garden hose or spray with mixture of non-detergent soap and water. Plant chives or garlic between plants.	Malathion. Spray when insects are visible on leaves. Repeat if necessary.
	Dark blemishes at blossom end of fruit.	Blossom end rot	Apply agricultural lime to elevate pH to 6.0 or 6.5.	
	General lack of vigor and yellowing of leaves.	White flies		Pyrethrum. Spray when flies appear and thereafter at 4- to 5-day intervals. Repeat 3 times.
Leeks and Onions	Shriveled unusable bulbs.	Onion maggot		Diazinon. Saturate furrow at planting time.
	Withered leaves with numerous white blotches.	Thrips		Diazinon. Spray as needed at 7-day intervals.
Lettuce	Sudden appearance of virus diseases.	Leafhopper	Plant crop in sheltered area.	Dimethoate. Spray heads when insects appear.
	Watery rot at base of plant.	Bottom rot	Plant seed in raised beds for improved drainage.	
Peas	Blossoms damaged. Egg clusters visible on young pods.	Pea weevil		Malathion. Thoroughly spray plants as they begin blossoming.
	Seed rots and fails to germinate or young seedlings wither and die.	Seed decay and damping off.	Use pre-treated seed.	Captan. Dust seed with small amount of powder before planting.
Potatoes	Damaged leaves	Colorado potato beetle	Crush egg clusters when visible and hand-pick adult beetles. Plant beans or marigold with potatoes.	Sevin. Spray plants when larvae first become visible. Repeat 2 or 3 times.
	Spotted leaves	Leaf fungus		Maneb. Spray when plants are 6 to 8 inches high and repeat at 7- to 10-day intervals.
Radish	Gouged and tunneled roots.	Root maggot		Diazinon. Drench furrow before sowing seed and again 3 to 5 days after seedlings appear.
Spinach	Small, white tunnels within leaf.	Leaf miner		Malathion. Spray leaf surfaces when damage is detected and repeat when necessary.

Vegetable Drying

Long before the appearance of the modern freezer, homesteaders kept vegetables through the long winter by drying them. Today most people freeze and can surplus food. But drying has some advantages that are hard to pass up. To begin with, dried vegetables are easy to package and store. Also, the simpler drying methods require less in the way of equipment.

The first step in drying vegetables is to prepare them properly. Select only unscarred, healthy produce for drying, then peel or skin. Cut up or dice in uniform pieces, avoiding slices that are too thin or too thick. Some vegetables, such as beets, carrots, corn, peas, pepper, and squash, retain their flavor and quality better if steamed 10 to 15 minutes before being spread out on racks to dry. Finally, drain vegetables and dry with a towel.

To sun-dry vegetables, place them on wire mesh or cheesecloth trays and expose to sun for two to four days, depending on weather conditions. To oven-dry, place the trays in an oven preheated to 150° for 4 to 12 hours, stirring occasionally. After drying, "cure" in a warm, dry room for a week or two. Place vegetables in a large container in a hot, dry room. Stir once a day.

Vegetable Drying Chart

Vegetable	Preparation for Drying	Dryness Test
Beans, Green Lima	Shell and steam 15 to 20 minutes or till tender but firm.	Shatters when hit with hammer.
Beans, Snap	Trim and slice lengthwise or cut in 1-inch pieces. Steam about 20 minutes or till tender but firm. Spread about ½ inch deep on trays.	Brittle, dark green to brownish
Beets	Trim off all but 1 inch of tops and roots. Steam whole from 30 to 60 minutes, depending on size, or until cooked through. Cool and peel. Cut in ¼-inch cubes or ⅛-inch slices. Spread not more than ¼ inch deep on trays.	Brittle, dark red
Carrots and Parsnips	Scrape or peel. Steam whole about 20 minutes or till tender but firm. Cut in ⅛-inch slices or 2-inch cubes, or shred before steaming. Spread not more than ½ inch deep on trays.	Very brittle, deep orange
Corn	Select tender, mature sweet corn. Husk. Steam on the cob for 10 to 15 minutes. Cut from cob.	Dry, brittle
Mushrooms	Peel large mushrooms. Dry whole or sliced, depending on size. No precooking necessary. If stems are tender, slice for drying; if tough, discard. Spread not more than ½ inch deep on trays.	Leathery to brittle
Onions	Select mature onions. Remove outer, discolored layers. Slice ¼ inch thick. No precooking necessary.	Brittle, light-colored
Peas, Green	Shell. Steam 15 minutes or till tender but firm. Stir frequently during the first few hours of drying.	Shatters when hit with hammer.
Peppers and Pimiento	Cut in ½-inch strips or in rings. Remove seeds. Steam 10 minutes. Spread rings two layers deep, or strips not more than ½ inch deep.	Pliable
Parsley and Other Herbs	No precooking necessary. Hang bunches of whole plant in a dry, warm place. When dry, crush leaves and remove stems. Store in tightly closed containers.	Brittle
Squash, Winter and Pumpkins	Quarter; remove seeds and pith. Cut in 1-inch strips; peel. Slice strips crosswise, ¼ inch thick. Steam 8 to 13 minutes till slightly soft but not sticky.	Leathery
Squash, Zucchini	Cut in ¼-inch slices. Steam 3 minutes or till tender but firm.	Brittle

Storage of Vegetables

Once that first snow swirls in to blanket your garden, it seems that nothing will ever break the grip of winter. But if you plan ahead and make provision for storing surplus vegetables, you can enjoy fresh crops practically to the Ides of March. Simply set aside an unheated corner of your cellar for a storage bin.

Protect your storage area from mice by surrounding it with wire mesh, and maintain a temperature of about 32 degrees for most vegetables. At the same time, try to keep a fairly high level of humidity by moistening the floor. Finally, keep the area dark and well-ventilated. (See the chart on the next page for storage recommendations for specific crops.)

Even if your cellar is small or inaccessible, don't rule out vegetable storage. Crops can be kept in a protected crawl space or in an outdoor pit. Just select a place protected from freezing temperatures. Outdoor storage means you'll have to brave cold and drifts to dig out vegetables. But all you need is a steel drum or other container that's sunk into the ground. Simply stack vegetables on top of straw bedding, placing additional straw between each kind of vegetable. Cover the opening with wood and straw. Finally, cap with a 6- to 8-inch layer of soil, and cover with waterproof material.

To ensure success, great care should be taken when sorting vegetables for storage. Avoid scratching or nicking outer skins, and check your location periodically so you can immediately remove any vegetables that start to deteriorate. Before storing rind crops such as winter squash and pumpkins, allow them to cure in the field a few days so their skins will harden a bit. If frost threatens, bring them indoors.

Storage Chart

Veg.	Storage	Temp. Deg. F.	Humidity	Special Helps
Dry beans and peas	Any cool, dry place	32°-40°	Dry	Leave beans and peas on plants until thoroughly matured. Spread out in a dry, ventilated place and allow to dry for 2 or 3 weeks. Shell and store protected from rats and mice in bags, cans, or jars.
Fall cabbage	Outdoor pit or trench	32°	Moderately moist	Place heads, roots up, in a trench 2 feet wide by 8 inches deep that has been lined with straw or hay. Cover with additional straw. Cap trench with a 6-inch layer of topsoil.
Cauliflower	Storage cellar	32°	Moderately moist	Raw storge is not always reliable. Store like cabbage. Or, cut the entire head, wrap in plastic, and place in the refrigerator.
Carrots and beets	Storage cellar	32°-40°	Moist	Place in 10-gallon crocks and cover with burlap or other material to maintain moisture. Carrots may be stored at higher temperatures by removing tops completely and storing in damp sand. Storage beets should have 1 inch of stem remaining.
Fall celery	Pit or storage cellar	32°	Moderately moist	Dig a pit 12 inches wide by 24 inches deep and store plants with root clump. Water plants and allow tops to dry. Construct a sloping roof with planks, poles, or old corn stalks. Cover with a layer of straw or hay.
Onions	Any cool, dry place	32°	Dry	Store only fully matured and dried onions. Do not store in the cellar. Arrange in well-ventilated, open-mesh or slatted boxes and place in the attic or in an unheated room.
Endive	Storage cellar	32°	Moderately moist	Follow the storage procedure recommended for celery. Tie leaves together to aid the blanching process.
Rutabagas, turnips, parsnips, salsify, and horse-radish	Outdoor pit	32°-40°	Moist	Parsnips, salsify, and horseradish may be left in the ground through the winter if mulched properly. Rutabagas and parsnips should be either waxed or buried in moist sand.
Potatoes	Storage cellar	35°-40°	Moderately moist	Destroy any blighted or damaged tubers. Temperatures above 40°F. will induce sprouting. Properly stored, potatoes will last through the winter. Store in darkness. If storage is too cool, potatoes become sweet. Hold at room temperature for 1 or 2 weeks before using.
Peppers	Unheated cellar	45°-50°	Moderately moist	Firm, dark-green peppers can be kept 2 to 3 weeks if properly handled. Pick just before frost. Wash and sort. Store in plastic-lined containers with 12 to 16 holes for ventilation. Temperatures below 40° F. will cause decay.
Pumpkins and squash	Storage cellar	55°	Moderately dry	Select uninjured fruits for storage. Cure at temperatures of 80 to 85° F. for 10 days. (Acorn squash need not be cured.)
Tomatoes	Cellar	55°-70°	Moderately moist	Select tomatoes from vigorous vines for storage. Remove stems, wash, and let dry. Do not wipe, since sand scarring may result. Store partially red tomatoes in separate containers. Green tomatoes should be sorted each week so ripened fruits can be removed.
Sweet potatoes	Storage cellar	55°-60°	Moderately moist	Handle with care, since sweet potatoes are easily cut and bruised. Cure for 10 days under moist conditions at 80 to 85° F. then move bins to a cooler area. Do not store at less than 50° F. or in outdoor pits.

The starburst umbels of dill make it a popular garden herb. Leaves are delicious in salads, while seeds can be used in pickling.

Herbs
For Flavor & Fragrance

Nowhere is our partnership with nature more evident than in the remarkable history of herbs. As easy to grow as weeds, herbs capture the imagination with their sweet and pungent scents.

In no time, whether by accident or design, herbs were given strange and magical powers. Some, like St. John's Wort, were gathered and hung over doors to ward off evil spirits. Parsley, however, had the opposite effect; non-germinating seeds were believed snatched by the devil. The Greeks on the other hand viewed parsley in a more generous light. Withered wreaths were placed on the head of the victor of the Isthmian games. And garlands were worn by guests at Greek banquets to promote peace of mind and a good appetite.

Herbs even found their way into Greek mythology. Daphne, fleeing the amorous advances of Apollo, appealed to the gods for help and was promptly changed into a laurel tree. The persistent Apollo took to wearing laurel crowns in consolation. The Romans, eager to absorb the best of Greek culture, adopted the laurel crown for their rulers and generals. Reports have it that Caesar himself valued his laurel crown above all else because it camouflaged his baldness, which was considered an unsightly deformity.

Through the ages, vegetables and herbs have been given medicinal qualities as well. European peasants, for example, believed that a potato kept in a trouser pocket would keep away rheumatism. But medicinal use of herbs gradually became more scientific until whole books were written on the subject. Some modern medicines have herbs as their original source. Quinine was extracted from cinchona bark, digitalis from foxglove, and morphine from the opium poppy.

But you don't have to be a medicine man to appreciate the joys of herbs. A mere touch of a leaf will fill the garden with a delicious aroma. Gathered at peak ripeness, leaves, stems, roots, blossoms, and even stalks can add interest to the simplest of meals. All you need is a handful of the commonly grown herbs to make your garden complete. One of the advantages of herbs is that they can be planted almost anywhere, in formal, classical patterns, or among flowers or vegetables. Or when winter approaches, lush herb gardens can be maintained on a sunny windowsill, as a host of herbs grow well as container plants. If you lack sun, grow potted herbs under lights.

Sun and Soil. The most essential ingredients for successful herb growing are full sun and good drainage. Almost all herbs are more compact in growth, produce more abundant leaves, and are richer in oils and flavor when allowed to thrive in ample sunshine. When planning your herb garden, look for a sunny site well protected from the freezing winds of winter. Avoid low spots, since frost tends to hover in valleys and depressions. And remember that the closer herbs are to the kitchen door, the more likely they are to find their way to the dinner table.

As for the soil, herbs do poorly if forced to grow in areas of excessive moisture. Rainwater should percolate easily through the soil, yet enough should remain to provide a continuous supply. When choosing a site, take a sample of soil in your hand and see if it crumbles easily. Or you can dig a shallow hole, fill it with water, and test the drainage by observing how long it takes for the water to disappear. If water is still visible two hours later, you'll have problems growing almost anything, including herbs. A dense soil can be improved by working in sand and by loosening the subsoil. (See Gardening Intensively, page 18, for additional methods of improving soil and subsoil.)

If all else fails, herbs do very well in raised beds where drainage conditions are ideal. (Check pages 20 and 21 for tips on constructing, cultivating, and planting raised gardens.)

Shade Herbs. There are a handful of herbs that will tolerate partial shade. If full sun is scarce, try sweet woodruff, which makes an exquisite ground cover because of its creeping growth and attractively patterned leaf whorls. Lovage, a vigorous grower popular in salads, soups, and stews, will grow in patchy shade, but a rich, fertile soil is necessary. The mint family, with its seemingly endless variety of fragrance and flavor, does especially well in the shade—so well, in fact, that their rank growth will threaten to crowd out neighboring plants if not kept under strict control. Chervil, ginger, oregano, parsley, and sweet cicely are other herbs that will grow in mottled or partial shade.

Annual Versus Perennial. Perennial herbs offer the advantage of coming up each year, while annuals must be planted from seed each spring. Chives, tarragon, woodruff, mint, cicely, catnip, marjoram, rosemary, sage, dandelion, and thyme are popular perennials. Some, however, will not survive harsh winters. Tarragon, marjoram, and rosemary should be snuggled under a thick mulch for winter protection. Other perennials, such as mint, are persistent creepers and will invade every nook and cranny of your garden. To control growth, simply start cuttings or nursery plants in metal cans with the bottoms cut out. Or rim the mint bed with metal edging pushed at least 6 inches into the soil. It's also a good idea to remove flowers before they set seed.

Annual herbs, which include dill, chervil, borage, coriander, fennel, basil, and parsley, are normally planted each season. Technically, parsley and dill are biennials, but are most often treated as annuals. Many of these annual herbs reseed themselves each year.

Harvesting Herbs. For peak flavor and freshness, pick leaves just before flower buds begin to open, especially if leaves are intended for storage. Try to do your harvesting during the morning hours. Place leaves on a rack to dry, and then store in airtight containers kept in a cool, dark place. For more detailed information on drying specific herbs check the individual herb entries beginning on page 86.

A handsome sundial completes this classical herb garden. Woolly thyme surrounds the base, while chives blossom at rear.

Traditional Herb Plantings

A traditional design, almost as old as civilization, consists of two intersecting paths about three feet wide. This plan can be enlarged or modified to fit your location.

Part wagon wheel and part goose-foot, this variation on a theme parcels space into attractively planted triangles. Plenty of sun and good drainage are essential.

The Roman nobility's idea of absolute luxury was a well-ordered garden gracing the entrance to their home. As they strolled along the leafy walkways bordering herbs and vegetables, they would ponder the day's events. Later, as gardening became more sophisticated, herb gardens grew in size and intricacy until patterns and designs took on as much importance as the herbs themselves.

No doubt, the ordering of plants into exact geometric designs resulted from the rank growth habits of many of the herbs. Perennials especially will straggle every which way if not kept in bounds with brick or stone curbing. At the same time, parcelling out the various herbs makes each specimen more accessible. A well-designed garden also promotes neatness—essential if prized herbs are not to suffocate from invasive weeds.

There are almost as many plans for herb gardens as there are herbs. But the simplest traditional design consists of two 3-foot paths intersecting each other at their midpoints (according to the ancients, the resulting cross would frighten off evil spirits). The four square beds may be bordered with brick or any other suitable material. As your enthusiasm for herbs grows, you can easily add to this basic plan by forming a walk around the perimeter or by extending the crossed paths. For a classic touch, place a sundial, statue, or decorative stone in the center where the walkways intersect.

Another popular pattern based on classical designs is the wagon wheel. Brick or stone sunk into the ground form the spokes and rim, while herbs are planted in the pie-shaped segments in between. Or, if you're an old hand at herb growing, you can try a knot garden formed by planting border herbs, such as thyme or germander, in continuous, intertwining, rope-like hedges.

Appearance is everything in the traditional herb garden. Trim walks to keep them neat and accessible, and use mulches to combat weeds and retain moisture. Cocoa husks or buckwheat shells are good choices for mulch.

75

Informal Plantings of Herbs

For many people, the term "herb" triggers thoughts of intricate gardens planned and planted with slide rule accuracy. But herbs have a fun-filled side as well. Allowed a modest amount of freedom, they can become delightfully shaggy, making the garden truly a place of rest and relaxation. The mints, for example, are often frowned on for their undisciplined growth. But a sea of spearmint crowding a lawn or walkway offers repeated bouquets of fragrance when trampled underfoot or nipped with the lawnmower. Creeping thyme or chamomile can serve the same purpose.

If available space is in short supply, remember that herbs are perfectly adaptable to container gardening. Set out plants in individual pots, or construct wooden "herb shelves" and fill them with soil.

Be sure to allow for proper drainage. Pots should be filled with a layer of pot shards or fine gravel which is in turn covered with an inch or so of peat or sphagnum moss. The rest of the container is then topped with soil mix. Water thoroughly to allow soil to settle, scatter seed over the surface, and cover with a thin layer of soil.

To conserve moisture, cover containers with glass or plastic. Since most seeds need darkness for good germination, keep pots in a dark place or cover with cardboard or newspaper. But as soon as tiny seedlings emerge, remove covers and place containers in a sunny location. Thin plants when they're about 3 or 4 inches high.

If you have your heart set on a smattering of your favorite culinary herbs such as chives, thyme, sage, parsley, basil, rosemary, and mint, you can plant a small informal garden near the kitchen door or next to the vegetable patch. A 7x12-foot section can accommodate as many as ten different varieties. Make sure the site is in full sun and that soil has good drainage.

Most of the annual herbs, including dill, basil, borage,

Perennial sorrel is a favorite seasoning for soups and sauces.

Fine, lacy leaves of fennel and mint contrast nicely with the foliage of container strawberries. Be sure to provide good drainage.

Flue tiles pushed into the ground make attractive planters, and at the same time keep herbs in bounds.

three years. In front of the sage, try equal amounts of parsley and summer savory. Along the front leg of the triangle, plant a border of chives. In the opposing corners, set out a plant or two of thyme.

Perennial herbs such as lemon balm, sage, mint, thyme, rosemary, chives, tarragon, and chamomile may be started from seed, but usually are propagated from cuttings or runners that are dug from other beds or purchased at a nursery. Once established, perennials will appear year after year. To rejuvenate plantings and contain growth, it's best to divide clumps every two or three years.

An ideal spot for cooking herbs, especially the annuals, is in and among vegetables. Since the vegetable garden is tilled each year, perennials should be placed elsewhere. Parsley and basil make excellent border plantings, while taller-growing dill and coriander can be sown between tomatoes or cabbage and broccoli.

When searching the backyard for a suitable place for herbs, don't forget their ornamental value. Many

have delicately formed leaves and numerous exquisite blossoms that can serve as an attractive setting for more showy flowers. Or, bushy herbs can be put to effective use as border plantings. Purple basil, for example, has unusually colored leaves that are both attractive, tasty, and fragrant.

Gardeners enamored with the traditional ground covers such as myrtle and pachysandra often overlook the value of low-growing herbs for those difficult shady places where grass can't get a foothold. Herbs are maintenance-free, natural spreaders, and offer unique scents in addition to blossoms. Chamomile, sweet woodruff, low-growing thyme, and germander are good candidates for trouble spots. Woodruff is especially handy because it thrives in the shade. Germander, however, needs sun and dry, well-drained soil. Space small species like creeping thyme 8 inches apart; big species need 12 to 15 inches. For faster results, purchase root starts. Most of these perennials will grow compactly if tops are clipped after they blossom.

marjoram, anise, coriander, and chervil, must be started from seed after the soil has thoroughly warmed. But you can get a head start on the growing season by starting seeds in flats indoors and then transplanting established plants outdoors after danger of frost has passed (see Getting Started, page 52, for how-to instructions on sowing seeds indoors). Or, you can locate a smaller herb patch in a neglected area between buildings or in an unused corner of the lawn.

An informal garden in the shape of a triangle with sides about 14 feet long can hold six or seven different kinds of herbs. At the back of the garden, plant the taller mints, then four or five sage plants. As sage develops, they will form small shrub-like plants that can be trimmed to a height of 8 inches in early spring or late fall. A perennial, sage ought to be replanted every

If space is scarce, interplant herbs with vegetables, or combine with flowers.

77

Growing Herbs Indoors

For gardeners hopelessly addicted to tinkering with plants and soil, the frigid winds of winter are dreaded more than the worst insect scourge. Even in antiquity, the Greeks and Romans, unblessed with the luxury of glass, found ways to keep green things going through the winter months by moving certain plants indoors. Once you have lingered by a window ablaze with leafy splendor while snow-filled winds growl just beyond the window panes, you'll never let another winter go by without having an indoor garden.

One of the easiest ways to launch an indoor garden is to start with a handful of herbs. Some can even be brought in from outdoors and given a choice location on a sunny windowsill. Or, you can purchase a couple of plants from a garden supply center; in no time, they'll be bushy enough to divide for repotting. If you'd rather start projects from scratch, start your favorite herbs from seed.

But always remember that indoor conditions are drastically different from those outdoors. Not only is "weather" different, but container gardening itself introduces a host of special considerations. Here are some basic requirements:

Sun. There's no escaping the fact that almost all herbs thrive in plenty of sun. It's not because they're fussy, but rather because most herbs originated in the sun-splashed Mediterranean region. A sunny window is a must, and since the sun sinks lower in the sky during the winter months, this means the window should face south.

Before choosing a location, compare windows to see which gets the most sun. If you can manage about four to six hours per day, you can count on an abundance of healthy herbs. Often you can improve light conditions by removing heavy drapes or trimming outside foundation plantings that have grown too tall. Some indoor enthusiasts juggle white paint, tinfoil, and other reflective materials in such a way that sunlight is increased dramatically.

Even if every window is shrouded in shade, don't chuck your indoor plans too hastily. Lush, aromatic herb displays can be easily and economically grown under artificial lights. A corner of the cellar or an unused closet are ideal locations, or garden on portable shelves. Some homeowners incorporate herb plantings right into their interior decorating plans. Most plants need about 20 watts of light per square foot. For best results, buy fluorescent bulbs manufactured expressly for indoor growing.

Temperature. One of the first maladies to hit indoor plants is drying out. Many homes, kept at constant high temperatures, become insufferable hotboxes for plants. It's a matter of simple arithmetic. Outside air moves inside with the same amount of humidity, but then it's heated, causing it to expand. Since the moisture content stays the same, the air becomes much drier—at times, actually pulling moisture away from plants, causing them to wilt and eventually die. So it's important to keep your indoor herb garden away from hot air currents. A good way to help maintain humidity for your herb garden is to mist plants occasionally with a hand-held mister made especially for the purpose. A tray or bowl of water placed in the vicinity of your plants also is helpful.

In terms of temperature, plants are hardier than you think they are. Ideally, temperatures for herbs should hover between 50 and 60 degrees, but temperatures as low as 45 degrees will not adversely affect plants. Remember that the temperature near a window pane on a bitterly cold night can get near the freezing point. Either insulate by placing a sheet of plastic over the window, or move plants away from the window when the weather turns extremely cold. Hang an inexpensive thermometer near plants to help you keep an eye on conditions.

Soil. When a plant is plucked

The closer herbs are to the kettle, the more likely they'll be included in the menu. Pots contain leaf lettuce, while thyme cascades from a hanging planter.

from the outdoors, stuck in a cup or two of soil, and then hung in mid-air, it's small wonder that it droops and turns brown. Suddenly snatched from acres of soil where water is always nearby, the plant must immediately adjust to living in air. Its roots, constantly cool outside, are abruptly forced to tolerate warm, dry conditions. So because of evaporation and the absence of subterranean water supplies, potted plants need much more water. Check the soil every day and water if necessary, watering herbs from the top, rather than from the bottom.

And since most herbs can't tolerate soggy root systems, make sure that adequate drainage is provided. Whatever container you use should have drainage holes where excess water can run out. If a decorative jug doesn't have holes, it's often possible to drill them. Or you can solve a drainage problem by putting a clay pot inside your favorite ornamental container. Place an inch or two of gravel in the larger container, and check every so often to drain standing water.

Plastic pots also have become popular, especially among nurserymen who appreciate their light weight and low cost. Trouble is, they don't "breathe" the way a clay pot does. As a result, moisture doesn't drain as rapidly, nor does air penetrate the soil as readily. Many gardeners also consider the soft, brick-red color and earthy texture of clay pots much more pleasing to the eye.

The ideal soil for herbs is rich in humus and at the same time porous enough to allow for good drainage. Beginning indoor gardeners find it much more convenient and less risky to simply buy commercially prepared soil mixes at a garden supply center. In small amounts, these scientifically constructed, artificial soils are germ-free and easy to use. If you anticipate large tubs or several window boxes in addition to a small army of individual herbs grown in separate pots, you might want to mix your own soil. The traditional ingredients are garden loam, peat moss, and sand mixed together in equal amounts. Since herbs do better in non-acid soil, add lime (about one cup per bushel).

Where there is sun and tender loving care, herbs will thrive. Here a leafy potpourri of thyme, chives, sage, oregano, rosemary, parsley, and mint transforms a work area into a miniature garden paradise. Pinching off tips of plants encourages bushy growth.

Planting and Transplanting. A quick way to get herbs on the windowsill is to dig up perennials from the garden and transplant them into pots for indoor use. Just before the first killing frost in the fall, dig plants from the edge of the bed, and place in pots and water thoroughly. In no time, plants will be ready for the family chef. But this doesn't mean they can be left to fend for themselves. The abrupt shift to indoor conditions with the attendant drop in available moisture will almost certainly spell doom for newly transplanted herbs. Water daily and shade from the direct heat of the sun.

When starting an herb garden, decide first on whether you want a working selection for the kitchen or whether fragrance is preferred. If you choose culinary herbs, plan on the basic eight: parsley, chives, sage, thyme, savory, basil, spearmint, and marjoram. For fragrance, plant mints, geraniums, and balm. Whatever you grow, the rich tradition of herbs can inspire years of happy experimentation.

Special Uses for Herbs

For Delightful Scents

The aromatic herbs have a charm and mystique all their own. Through the ages, they have been used in bath and breath fresheners, hair rinses, soap powders, room deodorizers, and even insect repellents. They are also some of the main ingredients in sweet-scented potpourris, sachets, and pillows.

To make a potpourri like the one at left, you'll need a collection of dried rose petals. Clip them during the summer and dry in a shady well-ventilated place. Store the dried petals in airtight containers until you're ready to make the potpourri, but be sure to stir them every few days. If you don't have a source of rose petals, rose geranium leaves can be substituted.

Next, crush a mixture such as lavender, orris root, tonka bean, sandalwood, lemon verbena, frankincense, and myrrh until you have a pleasing scent combination (orris root is a scent preservative that is available at most pharmacies). Thoroughly mix these ingredients with the dried rose petals, and cure in a covered container for five or six weeks, stirring the mixture every few days.

After curing, you can use the potpourri mix in sachets, or just store it in jars, opened occasionally to add fragrance to a room. Potpourris also can be placed in open bowls for a continuous fresh fragrance, but such a mix will not hold its scent for as long a time.

Perhaps the best way to make a potpourri mix pleasing to the eye as well as to the nose is to add some dried whole flowers for color. The bowl at left is filled with a potpourri mix attractively concealed beneath a layer of dried flowers. The flowers —camellia, pansy, alyssum, rue, apricot geranium, azalea, nastur-

tium, and forsythia—were dried with commercial drying powders.

Lavender sticks add a delightful fragrance to trunks, closets, and dresser drawers. To make a lavender stick, clip an odd number of lavender flower stalks just before they are completely open. Be sure to clip as much stem as possible. It's a good idea for beginners to start out with about eleven flower stalks.

Bunch the flower heads and tie the stems together just at the base of the flower heads. Use about a yard of narrow ribbon, leaving a long length on one side. Gently fold up the stems, one at a time, over the flower heads (stems will form a kind of "cage" with the flower heads in the center).

After the stems are folded, draw the long free end of the ribbon through the stems from inside, weaving in and out, and over and under the stem "cage," below. Be sure the ribbon stays flat, and that each weave is flush with the next. Continue weaving until the flower

heads are completely covered.

To keep the sticks from unraveling, tie the free end of the ribbon into a knot at the base of the woven head, and add a decorative bow over the tied knot. A rubber band placed around the free stem ends will keep them from spreading as the sticks dry. It also will make the stems less likely to break off.

To make a lavender pillow, above, simply remove the lavender flowers from their stalks and stuff and sew them into a dainty pillow, along with some powdered orris root as a scent preservative. Use pillows in closets, trunks, dresser drawers or in gift packages. Pillows retain their scent for several months.

Special Uses-- Homegrown Teas

The art of using herbs for teas is an age-old tradition that's currently enjoying a revival. Instead of buying your tea supply, why not try growing your own? Even a few plants of your favorite tea will give you a generous harvest. Or, set aside a little more space and grow two or more tea-yielding species. Then you can create your own blends, as your ancestors did.

To start your "tea garden," plant sage, comfrey, scented geranium, chamomile, catnip, lemon verbena, peppermint, or spearmint. The mints and catnip, particularly, will produce generously the first growing season after you set them out. In fact, these species will spread too fast in most gardens, so you'll have to protect yourself against invasive roots. Set starts in flue tiles or old baskets sunk in the ground.

Lemon verbena is not winter-hardy in northern areas, so treat it as a container plant. If you like the lemony flavor but want a perennial plant, set out lemon balm. It's a hardy species, and will grow happily in sun or shade.

Herb hobbyists will tell you that parsley is an underestimated plant, too often relegated to use as a garnish. Use parsley fresh at tea-making time, steeping stems and leaves in boiling water. Among other attributes, it's also high in vitamin C.

Another nutritious brew can be made from rose hips. Although the rose is not an herb, the hips, made into hot tea, can compete favorably with any real herb.

You can make teas from fresh-cut leaves, or from air-dried leaves or flower heads (use chamomile flowers, not leaves). Flowers should be harvested when the outer white petals of the flower curve backward and turn a slight yellow color. Clip and spread in a well-ventilated area until dry, or quick-dry in a pan over an open flame.

For the best harvest, wait until a sunny morning when the dew is off the leaves. Cut flowers or leaves with a sharp knife, leaving enough foliage to keep plants growing. Never cut back farther than the second set of leaves. In late summer, pot up cuttings of herbs such as scented geranium and mints to keep under plant lights or on a sunny windowsill. Then, all through the winter, you'll have fresh leaves.

You can harvest annual varieties more heavily if you know it's the last picking of the season. But perennial herbs need to build up strength before winter and should not be clipped any later than six weeks before the first expected frost. In cold climate areas, mulch perennial herbs with 2 to 4 inches of hay or leaves for winter protection.

Hang cut herbs in bunches to dry, or spread clipped leaves on screens or trays. Keep in an airy place out of sunlight until the leaves are crackly dry. If there is not enough air circulation around the tied bunches of herbs, they're likely to mildew and will no longer be usable. When herbs are dry, strip off the leaves, rub them to crumple, and store in airtight jars or tins away from direct light.

Seed heads are ready to harvest when the color turns to a greenish-brown and the stalks are dry. Harvest on a hot, dry day, and clip into a paper bag to prevent seed loss. Spread seeds on a cloth-covered tray in a dry spot. Dry for one to two weeks, then store in airtight jars away from light.

Making herbal tea is simple. Just use one tablespoon of fresh leaves or parts of leaves (or one teaspoon of dried leaves) for each cup of water. Bring the water to a boil, pour it over leaves, and cover the pot to let steep. After three to five minutes, strain and serve.

If the tea isn't strong enough, let the brew steep longer. Dried herbs give a stronger flavor.

Tantalizing scents, intricate leaf patterns, and unusual blossoms make herbs excellent candidates for companion planting.

Special Uses As Companion Plants

Too often, in the interest of increased efficiency, the home gardener insists on planting a vegetable checkerboard where each crop is grown in the same place year after year. Block planting may be simpler in the short run, but in time it can bedevil your garden with a host of problems. Cabbages will shrink and go limp for no apparent reason, corn borers will threaten to overrun the corn patch, or your prize potatoes will be smothered with potato beetles.

In nature, things grow willy-nilly rather than in neat, geometrically placed rows. As a result, insect populations are faced with limited food supplies and can seldom get out of hand. And today, experts agree that diversity is the best defense against bugs and disease. Through companion planting—combining specific plants so the beneficial qualities of one can be useful to another—you can keep the balance in your own backyard from tipping too far in one direction.

An unusual quality of herbs is their ability to repel insects. Since vegetables are often plagued by bugs, herbs can be a welcome addition. Marigolds, popular because of their colorful flowers, are especially effective. Planted among beans, they are said to discourage the Mexican bean beetle. Studies also have shown that large plantings have a way of destroying the root systems of certain starchy weeds. Nasturtiums can check aphids, striped cucumber beetles, and squash bugs, while tansy planted

Companion Planting Chart

Plant	Where to Plant	Possible Benefits
Beans or marigold	With or among potatoes	Discourages Colorado potato beetles
Chives or garlic	Among lettuce or peas	Deters aphids
Geraniums	Near grapes	Discourages Japanese beetles
Marigolds	With beans	Repels Mexican bean beetles
Nasturtiums	Throughout vegetable patch	Deters aphids, Mexican bean beetles, striped cucumber beetles, and squash bugs
Tomatoes	With asparagus	Discourages asparagus beetles
Euphorbia (gopher plant)	Scattered throughout garden	Poisonous to gophers and repugnant to many insects
Potato	With beans	Deters Mexican bean beetles
Radish	With cucumbers	Discourages striped cucumber beetles
Rosemary, sage, thyme, catnip, or mint	Among cabbage plants	Repels white cabbage butterflies
Rue	In or between vegetable rows	Bitter leaves are odious to insects
Tansy	Near cabbage	Helps reduce damage from cutworms and cabbage worms

with cabbage helps reduce cutworm and cabbage worm damage.

Some gardeners use herbs to lure injurious bugs to one spot where they can easily be eliminated. Plants of the mustard family are attractive to a number of insects, while African marigolds, woodbine, and evening primrose are said to attract Japanese beetles.

It will be some time, however, before the benefits of companion planting are scientifically established. So if your crops wilt under an intensive insect attack, chances are a chemical spray may be in order (see the Pests and Problems chart, beginning on page 66).

When making your garden plans, don't overlook the ornamental value of plants. Herbs especially can lend breathtaking beauty to your backyard garden. Their aromas and delightful leaf shapes are unmatched in nature. At the same time, herbs mixed with vegetables can turn a mundane garden into a showcase of color and texture.

For example, the broad, blue-tinged, relatively flat leaves of cabbage can be set off by the lacy leaves of dill. Or light-colored lettuce can be contrasted with dark, curly leaves of parsley. If a splash of color is needed, plan on a patch or two of marigolds or nasturtiums. Mint, sages, and rosemary offer delicious scents as well as attractive flowers. Or you can create a symphony in gray by arranging lamb's ears, santolina, sage, and lavender in eye-pleasing patterns.

Herbs are especially handy when it comes to planting borders or small hedges either along walkways or around flower and vegetable beds. Winter savory forms an exquisite low hedge that can be snipped to the desired height. Low-growing thyme, germander, hyssop, and dwarf sage also have compact growth habits that make them ideal for hedging purposes.

When a brick or stone path defies landscaping, try surrounding it with low-growing thyme or lamb's ears. And a stone outcropping can make a superb background for plantings of sweet woodruff, borage, sweet cicely, and the various mints.

But perhaps the greatest joy derived from herbs is the subtle flavor they impart to food. When planning your garden, make room just outside the kitchen door for the traditional kitchen herbs such as parsley, thyme, sweet basil, dill, rosemary, chives, oregano, and mint. All are excellent companion plants that can be intermingled with vegetables. Or set aside a small portion of the garden for a salad patch complete with greens, herbs, and cherry tomatoes.

ABCs
of
Herbs

Since before recorded history, man has boiled, chopped, ground, and dissolved parts of plants looking for the magic cure for everything from irregular heartbeat to insect bites. Blossoms, stems, leaves, and roots were thought to be endowed with mysterious powers. Today, of course, our approach to herbs is considerably more objective. But to the gourmet who fusses fitfully over his culinary triumphs, herbs are still the magic ingredient that can transform the ordinary into the unforgettable.

For the home gardener, herbs can mean even better-tasting vegetables, as well as delicious aromas and showy leaves and flowers. Keep in mind, though, that almost all herbs need sun and a fairly well-drained soil. Check each herb entry for specific growing instructions.

Garlic chives are herb perennials that grow to 18 inches tall and produce clusters of attractive white blossoms.

A

ANISE
(Pimpinella anisum)

Annual. Grows to 24 inches tall. Plant in a sunny location in spring after all danger of frost has passed. Seedlings do not transplant well, so seeds should be sown where the plants are to remain. When flower clusters turn gray-brown, harvest seeds by clipping into a paper bag. Store dried seeds in airtight containers out of bright light.

B

BASIL, SWEET
(Ocimum basilicum)

Annual. Grows to 24 inches tall. Start seeds indoors 6 to 8 weeks early, or sow directly outside in a sunny location after all danger of frost has passed. Harvest leaves before flower buds open. Keep plants pinched back for continuous growth. To harvest, pinch the leaves off the stem and spread in a well-ventilated, shady area until dry. Store dried leaves in airtight containers out of bright light.

BAY
(Laurus nobilis)

Perennial. Grows from 3 to 6 feet tall in a tub or pot, but in its native Mediterranean area, trees have reached 60 feet tall. Since growth from a seed or from cuttings takes months, it's best to buy small plants from the nursery. The plants require some sun, and well-drained soil. In southern regions, small clusters of yellow flowers appear. Bay is primarily an ornamental tree, but fresh or dried leaves can be used in long-simmering dishes. To dry the leaves, hang branches in a dark room where the temperature never gets above 70 degrees. When the leaves are just dry, spread each one flat between two cloths and weight down to flatten. Store in an airtight container. The plant will stand the first frost, but must winter inside in cooler climates. Bay needs morning or afternoon sun, and does best with cool 60-degree nights, good drainage, and high humidity. Indoors, place potted bay plants near a southern or eastern window. Mist occasionally and water when soil surface appears dry.

BORAGE
(Borago officinalis)

Annual. Grows to 18 inches tall. Sow seeds in early spring in a sunny location. Plants produce handsome starlike blue or white blossoms in early summer, and continue blooming until fall. Blossoms are very attractive to bees. Harvest young leaves as needed, and use blossoms to decorate beverages.

C

CARAWAY
(Carum carvi)

Biennial. Grows to 8 inches tall the first year, and to 24 inches the second. Sow seeds in a sunny location in late fall or early spring. After flower clusters turn brown, clip into a paper sack. Store seeds in an airtight container.

87

CATNIP
(Nepeta cataria)

Perennial. Grows to 36 inches tall. Plant seeds or divisions in fall or early spring. Grows well in full sun or partial shade. Plants spread rapidly. To harvest, pinch the leaves off the stem and spread in a well-ventilated, shady area until dry to the touch. Store dried leaves in an airtight container out of bright light.

CHERVIL
(Anthriscus cerefolium)

Annual. Grows to 24 inches tall. Sow seeds in a sunny location in late fall or early spring. Do not bury the seeds too deeply, since light is required for good germination. Keep plants pinched for continuous growth, and pick fresh leaves when needed. To harvest, clip whole plants before flowering and hang upside down in a shady, well-ventilated location. Store dried leaves in an airtight container kept in a dark room or cupboard. For wintertime production indoors, start seeds in pots in late summer or early fall.

CHIVES
(Allium schoenoprasum)

Perennial. Grows to 12 inches tall. Plant seeds or divisions in early spring in a sunny location. Pinch occasionally to encourage more vigorous growth, and divide plants every few years. Use leaves fresh or frozen, but dried leaves lose freshness quickly. In late summer, pot up a few bulbs and leave outdoors under mulch until frost. Then bring the pot inside and place on a sunny windowsill for an all-winter harvest. Garlic chives grow to 18 inches tall and have garlic-flavored foliage and delicate, snowy-white blossoms.

COMFREY
(Symphytum officinale)

Perennial. Grows to 30 inches tall. Plant seeds or divisions outdoors in

a sunny or partially shady location. Does best in soil that has a slightly alkaline pH. Harvest the plants before they flower. To harvest, spread leaves and roots in a well-ventilated, sunny spot until dry. Store in airtight containers. Use fresh young leaves in salads and tea.

CORIANDER
(Coriandrum sativum)

Annual. Grows to 30 inches tall. Plant outdoors in a sunny location after all danger of frost has passed. Seedlings are hard to transplant, so be sure to sow seeds where plants are to remain. When the flower clusters turn brown, harvest the seeds by clipping into a paper bag.

CRESS
(Lepidium sativum)

Annual. Grows to 12 inches tall. Also known as pepper grass, garden cress should not be confused with watercress, which is in the nasturtium family. Cress is an early spring quick-crop often used in salads or as an attractive garnish. Sow seeds thickly in the spring as soon as the ground can be worked. Plants germinate and grow very rapidly, so be sure to make successive sowings every week to 10 days to ensure a continuous harvest. Cress also can be grown indoors in pots on a sunny windowsill for an all-winter harvest. Leaves can be harvested as early as 10 days after planting. Cress also can be grown for its tasty sprouts. Several forms are sold for garden use, but the most popular are the flavorful curled-leaf varieties.

D-E

DILL
(Anethum graveolens)

Annual. Grows to 36 inches tall. Plant seeds outdoors in a sunny location after all danger of frost has passed. To harvest leaves, pinch off in early summer and quick-dry in a cool, airy place. Seal dried leaves in an airtight container as quickly as possible. When the flower heads turn brown, harvest the seeds by clipping into a paper bag. Store seeds in an airtight container.

F

FENNEL
(Foeniculum vulgare)

Annual; perennial in warm-climate areas. Grows to 48 inches tall. Plant seeds or transplants

outdoors in full sun after all danger of frost has passed. Use fresh leaves as needed. When the flower heads have turned brown, harvest the seeds by clipping the entire seed head into a paper bag.

G

GARLIC
(Allium sativum)

Perennial. Grows to 24 inches tall. Plant cloves outdoors in a sunny location in early spring. In late summer when the tops begin to turn yellow, bend them over with the back of a rake. Dig the bulbs when the foliage has turned completely brown. Store bulbs in a net bag, or braid the tops together to form a garlic "rope." Hang bags and ropes in a cool, dark, well-ventilated area.

GERANIUM, SCENTED
(Pelargonium sp.)

Annual; perennial in warm-climate areas. Grows to 24 inches tall. There are over 75 varieties with scented leaves, usually divided into six general categories: rose, lemon, mint, fruit, spice, and pungent. Start seeds indoors 10 to 12 weeks early, or buy transplants. Plant in a sunny location after all danger of frost has passed. Geraniums are most often grown in containers and hanging baskets. Harvest fresh leaves as needed. For dried use, clip leaves in the fall and dry in a well-ventilated, shady area. Store in airtight containers or use in nosegays, potpourris, and sachets. Pot cuttings in late summer and bring indoors for year-round growth.

H-K

HOREHOUND
(Marrubium vulgare)

Perennial. Grows from 1 to 3 feet tall. Start from seed in spring or fall, propagate with cuttings in spring through the summer, or divide large plants in the spring. Set plants 1 foot apart in full sun. Horehound does well in poor, dry soil, but cut plants back during growth to avoid burr-like blossoms in June through September. Bees are attracted to the small, white flowers and will produce an interesting-flavored honey. The fresh leaves have a musky smell that is lost in drying. The fresh or dry leaves can be used to make tea, and syrup made from the leaves may be made into candy or cough medicine. Dry leaves quickly by hanging in bunches in a warm location, then seal the dried leaves in an airtight container. Plants may be potted and brought indoors as winter window plants.

L

LAVENDER
(Lavandula sp.)

Perennial. Grows to 32 inches tall. There are three varieties: English or true lavender is the showiest and produces the most-fragrant flowers; spike lavender produces larger, more-fragrant leaves; and French lavender, slightly less popular, is grown as a bath fragrance. Start seeds of all varieties indoors 10 to 12 weeks early. Germination and survival rates are low, so be sure to sow extra seeds or plant divisions. After all danger of frost has passed, plant seedlings outdoors in a sunny location. Harvest fresh leaves as needed, and flower heads before they open. In cold-climate areas, mulch with 2 or 3 inches of leaves or straw for winter protection.

LEMON BALM
(Melissa officinalis)

Perennial. Grows to 24 inches tall. Sow seeds indoors 10 to 12 weeks early, or plant directly outdoors in a sunny or partially sunny location after all frost danger has passed. Do not cover seeds completely with soil when planting, since light is needed for proper germination. Harvest fresh leaves as needed for tea.

LEMON VERBENA
(Aloysia triphylla)

Perennial. Grows to 6 feet tall in a large container. After the danger of frost has passed, set cuttings 2 feet apart in a sunny, well-drained area. It's best to buy plants from a nursery, since cuttings are hard to root. Lemon verbena is deciduous, and will drop leaves in the fall or when brought indoors. It may be stored in a frost-free cold frame for the winter. Plants like a cool, sunny window with humid conditions. Feed frequently. The leaves have a scent of fresh lemons and may be used in

potpourris or to flavor drinks and stuffings. Dry the leaves rapidly in trays in the shade. Store in an airtight container.

M-N

MARJORAM
(Origanum majorana)

Annual; perennial in warm-climate areas. Grows to 12 inches tall. Sow seeds indoors 8 to 10 weeks early, then plant outdoors in a sunny location after all danger of frost has passed. Harvest fresh leaves as needed. After blossoms fade, shear back the entire plant several inches to encourage new growth. To harvest, hang plants in a warm, well-ventilated area until dry. Strip off leaves and store in an airtight container.

MINT
(Mentha sp.)

Perennial. The most common varieties are apple mint, orange mint, spearmint, and black peppermint. Height varies with variety, but ranges between 12 and 36 inches. Plant seeds or root divisions in early spring, and divide every few years to keep the plants vigorous. Harvest fresh leaves at any time. To dry, cut back stems to the second set of leaves just before the plants are about to flower. Hang stems in a well-ventilated, shady place, then store in airtight containers out of bright light.

O

OREGANO
(Origanum vulgare)

Perennial. Grows to 12 inches tall. Plant seeds in spring after all danger of frost has passed. Keep plants pinched back to encourage bushiness. To harvest, clip off leaves as the plants begin to flower, and dry in a sunny, well-ventilated place. Store in airtight containers. Cover plants with 2 or 3 inches of straw or leaf mulch during the winter in cold-climate areas.

P-Q

PARSLEY
(Petroselinum crispum)

Annual. Grows to 12 inches tall. Start seeds outdoors in late fall or early spring. Add some radish seeds to mark the row for the slower-germinating parsley. Harvest fresh leaves as needed. To dry, hang the whole plant in a shady, well-ventilated location. Crumble leaves and store in airtight containers. To freeze, wash thoroughly

in several changes of water, then blanch in boiling water for 10 seconds. Chill in ice water for 1 minute, then pat leaves dry with paper toweling. Freeze in small freezer bags, foil, or clear plastic wrap. In late summer, pot up young plants to keep on a sunny windowsill for wintertime use.

R

ROSEMARY
(Rosmarinus officinalis)

Perennial in warm-climate areas. Grows to a height of 4 feet. Rosemary will not overwinter in cold-climate areas. Start seeds midwinter indoors under lights, or plant stem cuttings. Seeds have a low germination rate. Use fresh leaves as needed. To dry, cut the plant back by half while it is in bloom. Dry leaves in a well-ventilated, shady area, and store in airtight containers. Where winters are cold, start young plants in pots from stem cuttings in late summer. Use a commercially packaged potting soil mix and water only when the soil surface feels dry. Indoors, plants rarely get over 30 inches. Place on an east or south windowsill for fresh use during the winter.

S

SAGE
(Salvia officinalis)

Perennial. Grows to 30 inches tall. Sow seeds outdoors in early spring. Plants may take two seasons to grow from seed to usable size, so it's a good idea to plant root divisions or stem cuttings. Use fresh as needed. To dry, cut back the stem tips when the flower buds begin to form and spread in a well-ventilated, shady place.

SUMMER SAVORY
(Satureja hortensis)

Annual. Grows to 18 inches tall. In early spring, sow seeds outdoors in a sunny location. Use fresh leaves as needed. To dry, cut the whole plant just before flowering and hang in a shady, well-ventilated area.

SWEET CICELY
(Myrrhis odorata)

Perennial. Grows 2 to 3 feet tall. Cicely grows best from self-sown seeds, since the plant needs to freeze and thaw to complete its growth cycle. Transplant seedlings in spring, or divide roots in fall or early spring. Plants do best in a shady, moist, rich soil. Harvest the anise-flavored green leaves or green seeds. Roots may be eaten raw or cooked. If plants are allowed to mature fully, they often will reseed themselves.

SWEET WOODRUFF
(Galium odoratum)

Perennial. Grows 6 to 8 inches tall. Seeds have an extremely long germination period. Make root divisions or stem cuttings in the spring or fall. The plants prefer shade and a moist, acid soil. Once established, the plants spread rapidly and require pruning. Harvest leaves while the plant is in bloom, and dry in a shady, well-ventilated place. Leaves are especially valuable for making traditional "May wine." The dry leaves smell like new-mown hay.

T-Z

TANSY
(Tanacetum vulgare)

Perennial. The tall stems reach 2 to 5 feet in height and should be protected from wind. Seeds are hard to establish. Divide well-established plants in early spring and set 1 to 2 feet apart. Since the roots tend to take over an area, they should be contained in a sunken, bottomless container. The plants do best in sun to partial shade and in well-drained soil. Since the leaves are strong and bitter, their culinary uses are limited. Dry the flowers upside down for use in fall arrangements.

TARRAGON
(Artemisia dracunculus)

Perennial. Grows to 30 inches tall. Sow seeds or plant stem cuttings in a sunny location in early spring. If you sow seeds, be sure to buy the German or French varieties. The commonly sold Russian variety is much less tasty. Divide established plants every few years to keep them vigorous, and keep plants mulched to avoid damaging the dense, shallow root system. Use fresh leaves as needed. To dry, cut the

plants back to a height of 4 inches in early summer and early fall. Spread in a shady, well-ventilated area, then store in airtight containers. In cold-climate areas, cover plants with a 3-inch layer of straw or leaf mulch for winter protection. Pot up young plants in late summer and place indoors on a sunny windowsill for an all-winter harvest. Water plants when the soil surface feels dry.

THYME
(Thymus vulgaris)

Perennial. Grows to 12 inches tall. Sow seeds indoors 4 to 6 weeks early, or outdoors after frost danger has passed. For faster results, plant stem cuttings or root divisions in a sunny location. Use fresh leaves as needed. To dry, cut plants back to a height of 2 inches just before flowering, and spread in a shady, well-ventilated location. Do not cut plants again. Store in airtight containers away from bright light. Thyme is very attractive to bees and can be especially useful planted near vegetable and fruit gardens to increase pollination. In cold climate areas, mulch the plants for winter.

A garden path lined with herbs in bloom—rue with its small yellow blossoms, red yarrow, and lavender.

At-a-Glance Guide to Using Herbs

	Apples	Beans	Beef	Bread	Butters	Cabbage	Cakes	Carrots	Cauliflower	Cheese	Chicken	Cottage cheese	Drinks	Eggplant	Eggs	Fish	Fruit salad	Game	Green salad	Jelly	Lamb	Liver	Mushrooms
Anise	■						■						■		■		■		■	■			
Bay								■													■		
Basil		■	■			■								■	■				■			■	
Borage						■													■				
Caraway	■			■		■			■														
Catnip																			■				
Chervil		■														■			■				
Chives														■	■								
Coriander	■			■															■				
Cress					■														■				
Dill		■						■		■						■			■				■
Fennel		■									■					■							
Garlic			■								■							■	■				■
Horehound					■								■										
Lemon Balm													■						■				
Lemon Verbena													■										
Marjoram		■									■												
Mint	■				■			■					■						■	■	■		
Oregano		■	■							■													
Parsley														■					■			■	
Rosemary		■									■										■		
Sage			■								■												
Summer Savory		■			■																		
Sweet Cicely													■				■						
Tansy			■																				
Tarragon											■				■								
Thyme			■					■										■					

	Apples	Beans	Beef	Bread	Butters	Cabbage	Cakes	Carrots	Cauliflower	Cheese	Chicken	Cottage cheese	Drinks	Eggplant	Eggs	Fish	Fruit salad	Game	Green salad	Jelly	Lamb	Liver	Mushrooms

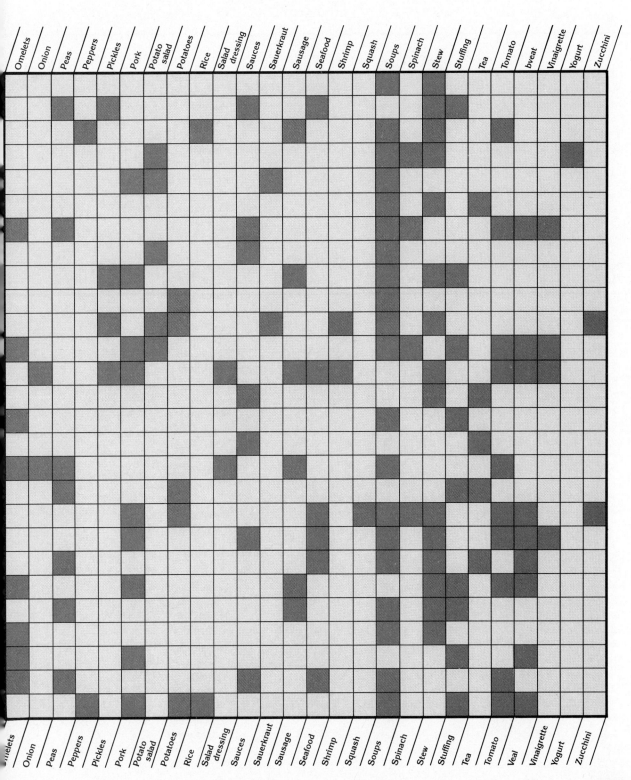

eaxxxxxxxxxxxxxxxxxxxxxxxxxxxxxxxxxxxxxxxxxxxxxxxxxxxxxxxxxxxxxx

Omelets · Onion · Peas · Peppers · Pickles · Pork · Potato salad · Potatoes · Rice · Salad dressing · Sauces · Sauerkraut · Sausage · Seafood · Shrimp · Squash · Soups · Spinach · Stew · Stuffing · Tea · Tomato · Veal · Vinaigrette · Yogurt · Zucchini

INDEX